# mastering
# peyote
# stitch

INTERWEAVE.
interweave.com

*editor*
MICHELLE MACH

*technical editor*
MINDY BROOKS

*art director*
LIZ QUAN

*photographer*
JOE COCA

*photo stylist and additional photography*
ANN SABIN SWANSON

*layout + design*
PAMELA NORMAN

*illustrator*
BONNIE BROOKS

*production*
KATHERINE JACKSON

 Interweave Press LLC
201 East Fourth Street
Loveland, CO 80537
interweave.com

Printed in China by C&C Offset

Library of Congress Cataloging-in-Publication Data not available at time of printing.

ISBN 978-1-59668-633-5 (pbk.)
ISBN 978-1-62033-085-2 (eBook)

10 9 8 7 6 5 4 3 2 1

## DEDICATION

*for Wally and Molly*

## THANKS

**Thank you** to Jean Campbell, Lisa Kan, Carole Ohl, Melanie Potter, Jean Power, Cynthia Rutledge, and Sherry Serafini. Amidst their busy teaching schedules, these talented *Beadwork* Magazine Designers of the Year created many of the beautiful and irresistible projects you'll find in this book.

I sincerely thank all of the wonderful designers, beaders, illustrators, photographers, and editors who contributed their talent, unmatched creativity, superb beading skills, and eagle eyes to this book. This includes Marlene Blessing, Bonnie Brooks, Mindy Brooks, Rebecca Campbell, Joe Coca, Karen Firnberg, Michelle Mach, Katie Nelson, Liz Quan, Ann Swanson, and Rachel Ure.

And last but certainly not least, I thank my extended family—this book wouldn't have been possible without their love and support.

The next time you're at a bead show or class, ask the beaders around you about their favorite technique and they'll probably tell you peyote stitch is their hands-down favorite. They might also tell you it's the first off-loom beadweaving stitch they learned. I actually came to beadweaving by way of daisy stitch: After studying the thread path of a tourist-shop bracelet, I spent a summer during my early teen years making daisy-chain bracelets. But it didn't take long for me to try my hand at peyote stitch, and I've never looked back. It's definitely my go-to stitch, meaning any time I sketch a new design or component, I almost always try the first sample with a peyote-stitch thread path. Plus, I love the meditative, repetitive, and soothing nature of peyote stitch.

Surprisingly, little is known about the exact origin of this popular stitch. You may already be familiar with the prevalence of peyote stitch (aka gourd stitch) in both past and present Native American beadwork. But did you know some of the earliest peyote-stitched artifacts date back to Ancient Egypt? And yet, centuries later, beaders still manage to come up with never-before-seen uses for this stitch.

One could never tire of this stitch because of its umpteen variations. With simple decreases and increases, a change in the number of beads strung, or a mix-up in bead size, you can turn a tube of loose beads into a fabric of beads that's anywhere from flat to three-dimensional. The projects in this book cover every peyote variation you can dream up.

In addition to my beaded creations, you'll find seven projects that showcase these limitless variations of peyote stitch. All-star contributors Jean Campbell, Lisa Kan, Carole Ohl, Melanie Potter, Jean Power, Cynthia Rutledge, and Sherry Serafini are known for their unique styles, mastery of beading, and time spent as *Beadwork* Magazine Designers of the Year.

Start with Carole Ohl's Buckle-Up Cuff. It's a great warm up if you're new to beading or if you've been beading for years and are seeking an easy-to-stitch contemporary design. Or, perhaps you're ready to explore the dimensional possibilities of peyote stitch, such as the beaded beads in Jean Power's Urban Skyline necklace or the gently curving leaves in my Walkin' After Midnight necklace. Looking for a statement piece that sparkles? Try Cynthia Rutledge's crystal-rich lariat or my Zigzag Zing crystal-rivoli bracelet. And if you love to create versatile seed bead components, make peyote-and-herringbone bead caps and mix them with brass chain and pearls in my Beaujolais necklace.

Turn to the Basics section for an overview of this beloved stitch, a guide to the terms and general techniques used throughout the book, and a refresher on the materials you need to get started. As the book progresses from flat to circular to tubular peyote stitches, check out each section opener for more detailed how-tos on each of these stitch variations. In the chapters that follow, combine peyote with other favorite stitches—including netting, herringbone, right-angle weave, and square stitch—and then learn a few must-know embellishments for adding a finished look to your designs.

I invite you to draw inspiration from each of the jewelry styles presented here, using them as a springboard for your own creations. Of course, I hope you fall in love with each and every project in this book. But, if your bead tray is full and you only manage to make your absolute favorites, I encourage you learn the techniques presented in each project—even if this means you only stitch a component or two.

Just when I think I know a stitch through and through, I'm amazed by what can be learned from new projects and innovative designers. The time you spend with your beads is special to you, so fall in love with peyote stitch all over again and start beading!

have fun,
Melinda

# basics

Dive right into the wonderful world of peyote stitch with this handy guide to beadweaving and jewelry making. Start off with an overview of bead types and the most common findings and tools. Do you sometimes feel as if we beaders speak our own language? Then don't miss the listing of must-know terms on page 18. Beading + Peyote 101 (page 19) covers everything from threading your needle to correcting errors and adding new thread. And last but not least, is a lesson on crimping, wireworking, and knotting (page 24) because, even if you bead strictly with seed beads, many of these techniques are necessary for designing and finishing your work.

## let's get started!

## BEADS
### seed beads
Seed beads are made of glass and come in a variety of shapes, sizes, colors, and finishes. They are sized on an inverse scale: the larger the number, the smaller the bead. Seed beads range from size 2° (largest) to 24° (smallest).

**Aught** describes a seed bead's size and is usually represented by a small degree symbol. The exact origin of this symbol is unknown, but it is thought to have once referred to how many strands of beads occupy an inch when lined up side by side. For example, eleven paral-lel strands of size 11°s (or eleven size 11°s laid side by side, not hole to hole) would equal an inch.

Most **Czech seed** beads are sold prestrung in 12-strand bundles called hanks. A typical hank of size 11° seed beads measures about 10" (25.4 cm) long (20" or 50.8 cm of beads per looped strand); hanks of size 13° charlottes, a faceted bead, are about 6" (15.2 cm)

## SIZE CHART

7 ◎ ▯▯▯▯▯▯▯▯▯▯
8 ◎ ▯▯▯▯▯▯▯▯▯▯▯
9 ◎ ▯▯▯▯▯▯▯▯▯▯▯▯
10 ◎ ▯▯▯▯▯▯▯▯▯▯▯▯▯
11 ◎ ▯▯▯▯▯▯▯▯▯▯▯▯▯▯
12 ◎ ▯▯▯▯▯▯▯▯▯▯▯▯▯▯▯
14 ◦ ▯▯▯▯▯▯▯▯▯▯▯▯▯▯▯▯

|← 1" →|

11° Japanese seed beads
About 17 per inch

|← 1" →|

12° Czech seed beads
About 21 per inch

long (12" or 30.5 cm per looped strand). One hank of size 11°s weighs about 35 to 45 grams. Manufactured in the Czech Republic, the beads on these hanks are temporarily strung on thin thread and must be restrung or transferred onto a stronger thread or wire. Czech seed beads are very round and donutlike and, when compared to cylinder beads and Japanese seed beads, are quite inconsistent in size. This isn't a bad thing—sometimes a bead that's a little too wide or a little too skinny will be just what you need.

**Cylinder** beads are perfectly cylindrical Japanese beads. Brands include Delica (made by Miyuki), Aiko and Treasure (made by Toho), and Magnifica (from Mill Hill). They are consistent in size and shape with thin walls and large holes. You'll find them in an impressively wide range of colors and in sizes 15°, 11°, 10°, and 8°. Aiko size 11°s run slightly larger than Delica size 11°s and are not easily interchangeable. Choose cylinder beads when your design requires precisely and consistently sized beads.

**Japanese** seed beads share characteristics of both Czech seed beads (because they are donutlike and round) and cylinder beads (because they are more consistently sized than Czech seed beads). Thanks to more consistent sizing, you'll spend less time culling these beads.

**Charlottes, true cuts**, and **one cuts** are seed beads with a single facet. This cut edge catches light, creating a sparkly look. Charlottes and true cuts are made in the Czech Republic. Although you'll hear these three terms frequently interchanged, technically, a charlotte is a size 13° single-faceted bead and true cut describes all other sizes of single-faceted Czech seed beads. Japanese beads shaped like this are commonly called one cuts (and thus beads with three facets are called three cuts).

**Hex cuts** have six evenly spaced, equal-sized surfaces that reflect light, resulting in a shiny bead. Hex cuts (and other shapes such as bugles, triangles, and cubes) are extruded as shaped beads, whereas faceted beads (such as charlottes) are cut by running strands of seed beads against a grinding tool.

**Bugle** beads are long tubes of glass. Bugles that range from 2mm to 11mm long are referred to by size, but be careful when you shop because Czech bugles and Japanese bugles are labeled differently (for example, a Czech size 1 is 2mm; a Japanese size 1 is 3mm); longer beads are sold by length, up to 35mm. To prevent thread breakage sometimes caused by the sharp ends of these beads, string one seed bead before and after each bugle, treating the three beads as one. Look for twisted and spiral bugle beads for added sparkle.

**Triangles** have three distinct sides. In general, Miyuki triangles tend to have rounded corners with round holes (though Miyuki "sharps" just hit the market at the time of printing); Toho triangles have sharper, more defined corners with triangular holes.

**Cubes** have four distinct sides and usually relatively large holes.

**Drops** (also called teardrops, magatamas, and fringe beads) are 2.8mm to 6mm teardrop-shaped beads with one hole and a bulbous end. Though you'll find these terms used interchangeably, Miyuki's magatamas are a little different than other drops: They have a less pronounced teardrop shape, a nearly round front profile and oval side profile, and are currently available in 2.8mm and 3.4mm. Miyuki's long magatamas are 4×7mm and come to a gentle point at the end.

**2-hole** beads are flat square beads with two holes that run parallel to each other. The thinnest types are made by Miyuki and called Tila. The thicker variety, called CzechMate, is made in the Czech Republic.

↑Czech seed beads ↓

cylinders ↓

hex cuts ↓

↓ bugles

↓ triangles

drops ↓

cubes →

charlottes →

9

2-hole ↓

peanut-shaped ↓

↓ aurora borealis
or iris finish

↓ matte
finish

↑ color-lined and
silver-lined

luster
finish ↓

↓ transparent

↑ opaque

**Peanut-shaped** beads, as their name suggests, are shaped like peanuts and have one hole in the center. They are distributed by Matsuno as "peanut beads," those imported directly from the Czech Republic are called *farfalle* (Italian for butterflies), and Miyuki's version is called "berry beads."

## seed bead finishes

The finishes added to beads drastically affect their color, often making the process of choosing colors complex. For example, a shiny red bead is no longer just red when treated with an AB (aurora borealis) coating. Thus, it's important to stitch a small sample to see how your beads will complement each other before diving into a large project. Plus, the way a bead looks inside its tube (or strung on a hank thread) can be drastically different from the way it will look when standing on its own. And it's not just about color—the balance of shiny and matte should also be a large consideration when selecting beads for a project.

**AB (aurora borealis)** and **iris** finishes give the bead surface a rainbow, somewhat oily-looking effect. This coating is quite stable compared to dyed and galvanized coatings.

**Matte** seed beads have a frosted appearance.

Hold a **color-lined/silver-lined** bead up to the light and you may find the bead to be a different color than you expected. A bead that looks solid green on your bead mat may actually be amber with a green lining. Beads with silver or gold linings have extra sparkle.

**Luster** is a general term for a shiny, glassy seed bead without special AB coating, matte finishing, or lining.

**Opaque** beads are solid colored and do not allow light to pass through them.

**Transparent** beads are primarily clear with a touch of color.

Beware of **dyed** and **galvanized** beads as their finishes may wear off.

Look for permanent galvanized and Duracoat beads, and ask your bead vendor about the coating's durability. Otherwise, after wearing your jewelry a few times, you may end up with a design made of only white or silver beads. Some beaders finish their work with clear acrylic spray (such as Pledge Floor Finish with Future Shine) to protect the coatings, but, if you choose this route, go lightly so you don't end up with a sticky piece of jewelry.

## rivolis, fancy stones, and chatons

A **rivoli** is a holeless, round crystal faceted to a point on both the front and back. **Chatons** are flat on the front, faceted to a point on the back, and typically smaller (1.3mm to 12mm) than rivolis. Holeless, faceted crystals found in shapes other than round are referred to as **fancy stones**. All are commonly available with a foil backing added to enhance the color and sparkle of the crystal. To incorporate these holeless elements in jewelry designs, beadweavers use seed beads to create bezels that surround the outside edges and sometimes the backs.

## cabochons

Often called a "cab," a **cabochon** is a flat or domed glass, stone, plastic, ceramic, crystal, etc., element with a flat bottom and no holes. They are most commonly glued to a beading foundation and beaded around or bezeled with seed beads.

## crystals

Crystals come in various sizes, shapes, and colors and are almost always faceted. Use beading wire or braided beading thread when stringing crystals because the sharp edges of the holes in the beads may cut through nylon beading thread. The two most popular manufacturers of these leaded glass beads are the Austrian company Swarovski and the Czech company Preciosa.

dyed →

← permanent galvanized

↓ chatons

fancy stones ↓

↓ cabochons

rivolis ↑

pressed glass →

↑ stones

← fire-polished

lampwork ↓

↓ freshwater pearls

↑ crystal pearls

← crystals

## other glass

**Fire-polished** beads are glass beads (generally from the Czech Republic) that are faceted to catch light and often have a surface finish applied to them for extra sparkle. Because of the large number of facets, fire-polished rounds tend to be slightly oval in shape. Fire-polished beads are an affordable alternative to crystals.

**Pressed-glass** beads (also generally from the Czech Republic) are made by pressing glass into molds. They come in a variety of colors, sizes, and shapes, including rounds, flowers, leaves, and more.

**Lampwork** beads are artisan-made beads created by working hot glass rods over a flame (in the old days, a lamp; today, a propane torch).

## pearls

**Freshwater pearls** are cultured in inland lakes and rivers. These are genuine pearls cultivated by inserting irritants into farmed mussels to stimulate their production; nacre coating is formed around these irritants, resulting in unevenly shaped pearls. Freshwater pearls are offered in innumerable sizes, shapes, and colors.

**Crystal pearls** are imitation pearls made by Swarovski and others and have a crystal core coated with a thick pearl-like substance. They are perfectly shaped and have a weight similar to that of genuine pearls. And unlike freshwater pearls, they have uniform holes.

## stones

Stones are available in a wide range of color, size, cuts, and quality. The holes can be tiny and require a small (size 13 or 15) beading needle. If the edges are sharp, be sure to use a durable thread such as FireLine. Because it's common for lower-priced stones to have inconsistently drilled holes, I often buy twice as many strands as I think I might need. Or, try adjusting the holes yourself with a bead reamer.

11

← thermally bonded thread

↓ beading foundation

↗ braided beading threads

Ultrasuede →

↑ nylon beading thread

thread wax and conditioner →

## FINDINGS
### beading thread

Regardless of which type of thread you prefer, always be sure to choose a color that closely matches your beads. Your beads are meant to be the star of your project, and thread is merely the underlying structure. If you're ever unhappy with the color of exposed threads, you can try coloring them with a fine-point permanent marker.

**Braided beading thread** is a highly durable synthetic thread made of many fine strands braided together. Brands include PowerPro, Berkley's FireLine, Beadalon's DandyLine, and The Bead-Smith's Spiderwire. Many were first designed for the fishing industry, so you'll often see them sized in terms of "pounds test" (meaning the number of pounds of pressure a single thread can withstand before breaking). The lower the pound

test, the thinner the thread. Many beaders find 6 lb test to be suitable for most beadweaving projects. If your project requires many passes through size 15° beads, consider using 4 lb test. Because of its resistance to fraying and strength, this thread is a great choice for beading crystals. Another nice feature is that it doesn't stretch. Most brands are only manufactured in two to three colors—smoke, crystal (white), and bright green.

WildFire by Beadalon is a durable, **thermally bonded beading thread** with no stretch. Available in two sizes, .006 and .008", this thread will not fray and cannot be pierced with a needle. I've found pieces made with this thread to be a bit stiff, making it a great choice for beaded ropes or other pieces of beadwork that you want to hold their shape.

Nymo and C-Lon **nylon beading threads** are available in a wide range of

colors, making it easy to ensure the color of your thread always blends in with your beads. These threads are also available in several sizes—ranging from 000 (very fine) to G (the heaviest), with sizes 00, 0, and A–F in between. Nylon thread does have a tendency to stretch over time, so it's always a good idea to give the thread a little pull to remove the stretch before making your project. Be sure to protect against fraying with thread wax or conditioner. The fewer passes a thread has through beads, the less it is likely to fray, so consider using shorter lengths of this type of thread. Also made of nylon, One-G is a strong thread manufactured by Toho. In my experience, it is less likely to stretch and fray than other nylon threads. Its size is similar to Nymo B.

### thread wax and conditioner

**Beeswax, microcrystalline wax,** and **thread conditioner** (Thread Heaven) are all used to protect your thread from wear and tear. They can also help prevent tangling, especially when working with nylon thread. Microcrystalline wax seems to be a favorite among beaders because it goes on lightly, doesn't ball up, and isn't sticky (like beeswax can be). To apply any of these thread protectors, sandwich the thread between the wax/conditioner and your index finger and thumb and pull the thread. If desired, repeat once or twice more. When applying additional coats, it's a good idea to run the thread between your fingers to smooth out any excess wax/conditioner. If working with nylon thread, you can also prestretch it at this stage. Wax/condition your thread if your project calls for a long thread that passes through beads many times or through rough- or sharp-edged beads such as crystals. And if you have trouble holding tight tension, waxing/conditioning is a must. For other projects, it's a matter of preference.

### bead embroidery materials

Lacy's Stiff Stuff is the most popular **beading foundation** for bead embroidery. It can be dyed with fabric dye

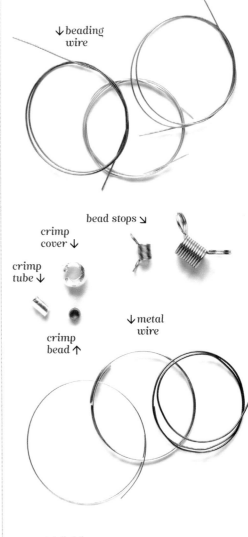

↓ beading wire

bead stops ↘

crimp cover ↓

crimp tube ↓

crimp bead ↑

↓ metal wire

to match any project, never stretches, won't snag your thread, is easy to stitch through, and is thick enough to support heavy cabochons. Use clear jeweler's cement (such as E-6000) to secure cabochons to the foundation before bezeling.

**Ultrasuede** is used to add a clean, professional look when finishing the back side of a beading foundation. Adhere it with white craft glue (such as Aleene's Tacky Glue).

## beading wire

This wire is a strong, flexible stringing material made of multiple thin wires (usually steel) that have been coated with nylon. The more strands of wires used, the more flexible the beading wire. This wire is most commonly secured with crimp tubes and crimp beads. Sizes .014 and .015 are great for lighter projects and best used with 1mm or 1×2mm crimp tubes and micro crimping pliers (see more on crimping pliers on page 17). Sizes .018 and .019 are great for medium-weight to heavy projects; use with 2mm crimp tubes. Be sure to check the wire manufacturer's size recommendations when pairing wire with crimp tubes.

**Bead stops** are springlike or cliplike findings that temporarily snap onto the end of beading wire to prevent spills while stringing. The smaller versions can be used in the same manner on beading thread to replace the need for stop/tension beads.

## crimping findings

A **crimp tube** is a small cylinder of metal (most often sterling silver, gold-filled, brass, or copper) that is manipulated with wire crimping pliers to secure beading wire to a finding.

**Crimp beads** serve the same purpose as crimp tubes, but are round, and are flattened using chain- or flat-nose pliers. Crimp tubes provide a more secure connection when attaching beading wire to a finding; crimp beads are best for "floating" beads on wire.

A **crimp cover** is a hollow, partially opened C-shaped bead that wraps around a crimp tube or bead to conceal it, giving jewelry a clean finishing touch.

## metal wire

**Hard, half-hard,** and **dead-soft** are terms that refer to the "temper" (hardness or softness) of the wire. Half-hard is most commonly used for creating wrapped-loop links and dangles. If you have just one temper in your bead stash, make it half-hard because it is flexible yet strong. Wire is naturally "work hardened" through manipulation; if overworked, the wire will become brittle and break.

**Craft wire** is copper wire that has been permanently coated with a colored finish. This wire tends to be soft and the color coating can chip, so use light pressure when wireworking. Or, work with nylon-coated pliers or pliers covered in painter's tape to minimize marring the wire.

**Gauge** is used to indicate the thickness of the wire. The most versatile wire sizes for making simple wrapped loops and links are 22- and 24-gauge. Use a thicker wire (the lower the number, the thicker the wire) if making your own clasp hooks.

## metal finishes

**Gold-filled** beads and findings are made of base metal (an inexpensive, nonprecious metal) that is bonded with a layer of gold that must be at least 10k gold and equal to at least 1/20 of the whole piece's weight.

**Gold-plated** materials are bonded with a layer of gold that must be at least 10k—the same requirement as gold filled. The difference is that the layer need not be 1/20 of the piece's weight; it can be much thinner.

**Fine silver** beads and findings contain 99.9 percent pure silver. Crafters can make their own fine silver beads with Precious Metal Clay (PMC) or Art Clay Silver, a substance that, when heated at

metal finishes

↓ filigrees

clasps

hook-and-eye →

toggle →

← s-hook

← box

↑ lobster

↑ snaps

tube →

↓ spring ring

↓ bead caps

↑ cones

a high temperature, releases stabilizers and leaves behind only pure silver.

**Silver-plated** refers to a base-metal component coated with fine silver.

**Thai silver** beads are handmade in Thailand by the Karen hill tribe. Thai silver is 95 to 99 percent pure silver.

**Sterling silver** beads and findings are 92.5 percent pure silver and 7.5 percent copper. Look for the "925" designation stamp on your components and jewelry.

**Brass** is composed of copper and zinc. "Raw" brass describes components with a goldlike appearance, and "natural brass" components have a darker, bronzelike finish. "Antique brass" is a shade somewhere in between the two but isn't necessarily vintage.

**Pewter** components are made of an alloy of tin (mostly), copper, and antimony. They are sold raw or plated with other materials.

## filigrees

**Filigrees** are metal components, such as pendants, beads, connectors, and links that feature lacelike ornamental openwork. They are available in numerous metals and finishes.

## clasps

**Toggle clasps.** These clasps have a bar on one side and a ring on the other. Since the bar must pass through the ring when attaching the necklace or bracelet, be sure to string at least ½" (1.3 cm) of small beads at the end of the strand before the bar.

**Tube clasps.** Found with either a long bar or a set of loops on each side, these tubular clasps are great for finishing beadwoven designs because of their clean profile. One half slides inside the other, and most styles have small magnets in the ends to help secure the closure. When attaching, be sure the ends will align when closed.

**S-hook clasps.** Made of an S-shaped wire permanently attached to a jump ring on one side, the S closes through a second jump ring on the opposite side.

**Hook-and-eye clasps.** These clasps have a J-shaped hook on one side that connects to a loop (or ring) on the opposite side. You can find small hook-and-eye sets sold in the sewing notions department at craft and sewing stores.

**Box clasps.** Shaped like a rectangle, square, or circular box on one end, these clasps have a bent metal tab on the other end that snaps into the box under its own tension. The tops often have stone, glass, pearl, filigree, or other decorative inlays, and the ends often have numerous metal loops (and sometimes jump rings) to accommodate multiple strands.

**Lobster clasps.** These (often small) closures open and close like a claw and are great for connecting jewelry to chain.

**Spring ring clasps.** Most commonly seen in sterling silver or gold-filled, these small round clasps open and close with a small tab that slides an inner wire in and out of its hollow core.

**Snaps.** Snaps are also sold as sewing notions but are great for beadweaving projects. The larger the snap, the stronger the closure. If your design calls for small snaps, try to incorporate several for added security. They are a great option if you desire a concealed, inconspicuous clasp. Sew them to beadwork just as you would to clothing, making several passes up and down through each opening. Pass through adjacent beads when possible, but, if needed, you can sew between beads, looping around threads of the beaded base. Backing each snap with a small piece of Ultrasuede will also secure their connection.

**Hook-and-loop clasps.** This sewing notion, best known as Velcro, is gaining popularity with beaders. This inexpensive material can be cut to accommodate any design shape. Use a pin to occasionally remove any lint that collects in the hooks and loops, and the closure should remain strong for years. Attach the closure to your beadwork using a new thread, so in the event you need to replace a worn piece of Velcro, you won't need to redo any bead stitches.

## caps and cones

**Bead caps** are decorative metal cup-shaped elements strung snugly against the top or bottom of a bead.

**Cones** are cylindrical findings that taper to a point at one end. They are great for neatly gathering the ends of multiple strands or covering the end of a beaded rope. Use at least 2" (5.1 cm) of gauged wire and form a wrapped loop that attaches to the end of your design. Use the wire end to string the wide end of the cone to cover the ends of the strands (or rope), then form a second wrapped loop that attaches to a clasp. Large bead caps can be used in the same manner.

## chain

**Chain** is available in a multitude of finishes, sizes, and shapes, including oval, round, short-and-long, and more. Most often the links are soldered and must be cut open. However, if the links are already split (unsoldered), they can be opened and closed like jump rings and no links will be wasted. Chain is measured by the size of an individual link.

## earring findings

**Ear wires** and **posts** are available in a number of styles and finishes. If purchasing posts, remember that the backs (or "ear nuts") are often sold separately.

## pins

A **flat-end head pin** is the most common style of head pin. When a bead is strung on one, the flat end sits flush against the hole in the bead. If the gauge is not indicated, it is probably 24-gauge; this gauge is strong yet thin enough to accommodate most beads. Head pins are often used to wire-wrap a

dangle to a piece of jewelry. A **ball-end head pin** has a round, instead of flat, end. **Eye pins** work like head pins, but have a simple loop at one end so that they may be connected to other design elements.

## rings

**Jump rings** are small, usually circular or oval pieces of wire used to connect jewelry components to each other. Most jump rings are unsoldered (called open), meaning they are severed and can be opened and closed to string components. Some are soldered (called closed), meaning they cannot be opened and closed, only linked to. When attaching beading thread to a jump ring, use a soldered ring at every possible chance to avoid the likelihood of the thread escaping the ring.

**Split rings** are similar to key rings: two overlapping loops of wire prevent the ring from being pulled open. Thus, they are a great choice if attaching beading thread to a ring.

## TOOLS

### work surface

A **bead mat** is a necessity to prevent beads from rolling off your work surface. The best are made of Vellux—consider buying a blanket and cutting it into mats for all of your beading friends!

I don't go anywhere without my **portable bead studio**. To make one, find a nice box that's at least 8" × 11" × 2" (20.3 × 27.9 × 5.1 cm), fill it with your project pattern, beads, needles, extra needles, a way to store broken needles, scissors and/or thread burner, notepad and pencil, thread wax/conditioner, bead mat, small ruler, and chain- or flat-nose pliers. You never know when you'll be called in for a long meeting or be sitting in a waiting room.

A **design board** is a valuable tool that prevents beads from rolling around your work surface. Most have semicircular grooves in the shape of a necklace or

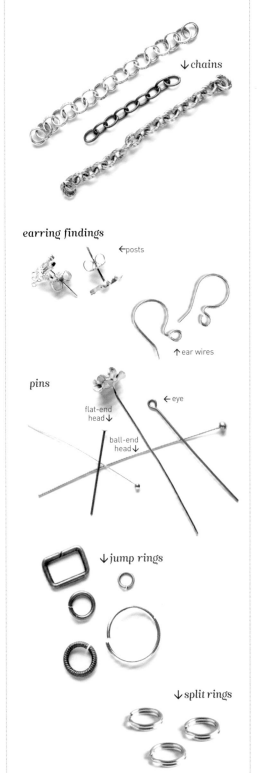

↓ *chains*

*earring findings*

← posts

↑ ear wires

*pins*

← eye

flat-end head ↓

ball-end head ↓

↓ *jump rings*

↓ *split rings*

15

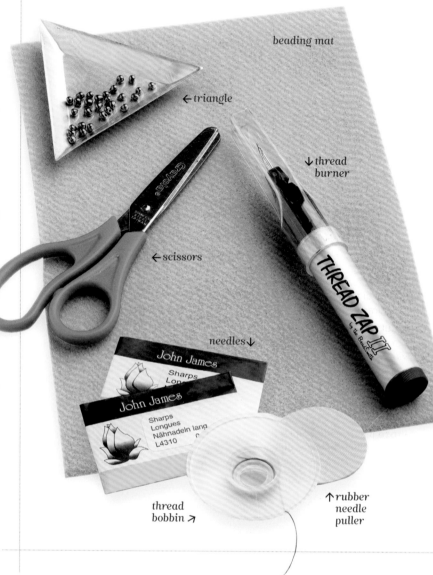

**beading mat**

← triangle

↓ thread burner

← scissors

THREAD ZAP

needles↓

John James

Sharps Lon

John James

Sharps
Longues
Nähnadeln lang
L4310

thread bobbin ↗

↑ rubber needle puller

bracelet that allows you to visualize a design before it is strung. Although this is not a required tool for beadweaving, you may find it very helpful when designing your own jewelry.

## needles

Stock up your stash with size 12 and 10 **beading needles**—these two sizes accommodate most beading projects you'll encounter. The larger the number, the thinner the needle. Never force a needle through your beads. Instead, switch to a thinner needle, such as a size 13 or 15, when navigating tight spots or you might break beads. It's not uncommon for thin needles to break; just be sure to safely dispose of the broken parts.

**Sharps** measure about 1" (2.5 cm) long (much shorter than the standard 2" or 5.1 cm long beading needles) and therefore can be hard to hold when stitching. However, they can be very useful when stitching in tight spots.

**Rubber needle pullers** are small (1" or 2.5 cm) discs of textured rubber—much like what you use to open tightly lidded jars in the kitchen—that can help you get a grip on the needle. Look for these at your needlework or craft store.

## thread bobbin

To help control a long tail thread while stitching, or to keep an in-progress project's thread from tangling during storage and transportation, wrap it around a **No-Tangle** bobbin. The snap-down side will keep the thread from raveling.

## triangles

A small metal **triangle** is a simple yet valuable tool for quickly cleaning your bead mat. It is the perfect scoop for picking up beads, and the pointed corners make it easy to sort beads and pour them back into their tubes. You can also pour your beads back in the tubes by using a rolled up conical piece of paper that acts like a funnel.

## bead storage

How you choose to store your beads comes down to personal preference. I have a rolling cabinet with several drawers that hold my seed beads sorted by color. Some beaders sort by bead type, others sort by size. You may prefer clear plastic tackle, thread-storage, or hardware-storage boxes (check the needlework, fishing, and tool departments at your local stores). They allow you to see your beads without cracking open the lid and are easy to transport. Plus, the caps on seed bead tubes can pop off, making

solid boxes where the tubes won't slide around or get crushed ideal. When you store hanks, tie a knot around the last bead on the hank thread to prevent the rest of the beads from sliding off.

## cutting tools

Be sure to keep your **scissors** sharp. The cleaner the cut on the end of the thread, the easier it will be to thread your needle. Interestingly, children's Fiskars scissors are great at making a clean edge when cutting braided beading threads such as FireLine.

A **thread burner** is great for cutting threads close to beads. Not only does this tool let you get in close to the beads, making sure no little thread tail is showing, but it also lightly melts the end of synthetic threads, creating a ball that keeps the final knot from coming untied. Don't use a thread burner when cutting thread off the spool, otherwise the small ball of melted thread will make threading the needle difficult. Here's a tip: When you're ready to end a thread, knot it, weave through a few beads, and "cut" the thread with the thread burner 1/16" (.2 cm) away from the last bead exited. Then chase the tiny tail to the base of the beadwork, melting it and encouraging it to ball up.

**Wire cutters** (or **flush cutters**) are used to cut both gauged wire and beading wire. Their sharp edges ensure that no burrs are left on the trimmed ends of the wire.

## pliers

The inside jaws of both **chain-** and **flat-nose** pliers are flat and smooth. However, the outside edges of chain-nose pliers are round on the top and bottom, and flat-nose pliers are flat on both edges. Chain-nose pliers taper toward the tip, making them great for working with small findings and in tight spaces; flat-nose pliers are wider, giving you more gripping power. Projects that direct you to open and close jump rings will require two pairs of chain- or flat-nose pliers. Use either to help gently push, pull, and/or wiggle your needle through tight spaces. Just be sure you aren't using the pliers to pull so hard that you break a bead; remember, it's best to switch to a smaller needle to ease stitching.

A pair of pliers is also handy if you notice a stitching error caused by adding too many seed beads. See Correcting Errors (page 20) for more information.

**Round-nose** pliers are used to make loops and curls with wire. Their conical jaws taper toward the tip, creating many loop-size options. If a large loop is desired, position the wire near the base of the jaw; for small loops, work the wire at the tips.

**Crimping** pliers have two notches used to secure crimp tubes on beading wire: one notch is used to flatten crimp tubes and the other is used to fold the tube in half. They are available in three sizes; pliers that accommodate 2mm tubes are the most common.

## design tools

A quick Internet search for **peyote graph paper** will yield many options for free downloadable design paper. Most commonly found for flat peyote designs, charts are also available for circular peyote designs. Simply print the graph paper, color in a design, and follow the chart bead by bead as you stitch *(fig. 01)*.

To help mark your stitching progress, photocopy the pattern and cross out rows as you work. Or, place the pattern in a clear plastic sheet protector and blackout completed sections with a permanent marker. You can also track progress directly on the pattern with a pencil and erase the marks when done. By cutting a wavy edge that matches the peyote up and down beads on a piece of paper or sticky note, you can cover up progress row by row.

**Photocopiers** are great for testing the scale and overall look of any design. This tool was invaluable when designing my Happy-Go-Lucky Links necklace. After beading just one oval ring, I made several copies of it. I then cut the copies out and played around with several ways to arrange the rings with the lampwork rounds. Finally, I taped them all together to determine the overall length and started beading the rest of the project. This is one of my favorite ways to design. See the "Designing Beadwork" sidebar on page 103 for more design tips.

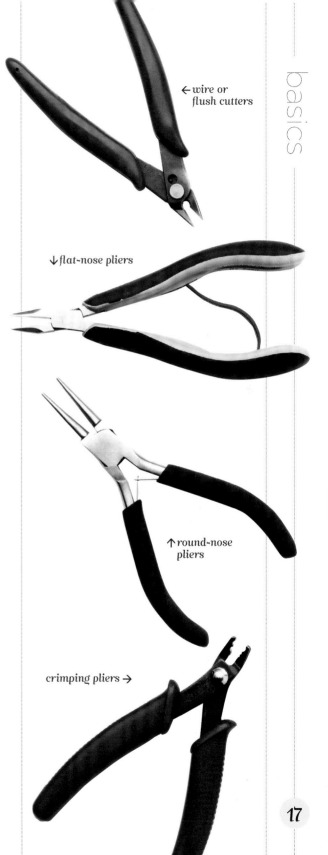

←wire or flush cutters

↓flat-nose pliers

↑round-nose pliers

crimping pliers →

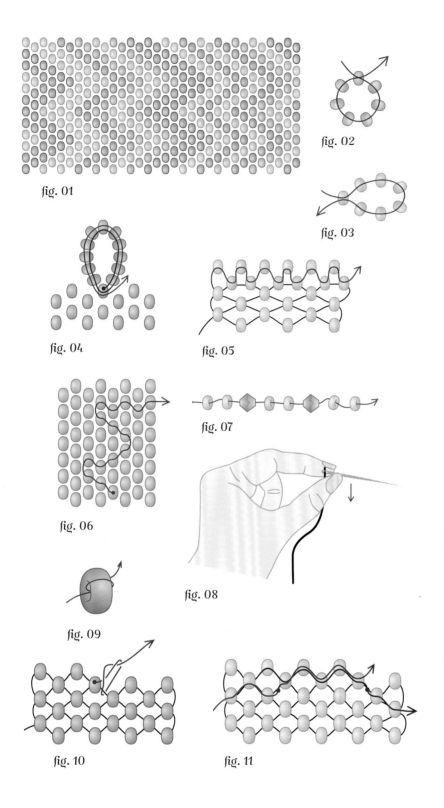

fig. 01

fig. 02

fig. 03

fig. 04

fig. 05

fig. 06

fig. 07

fig. 08

fig. 09

fig. 10

fig. 11

## MUST-KNOW TERMS

**Conditioned vs waxed thread.**
Conditioned thread is lightly coated with a synthetic thread conditioner, usually Thread Heaven (in the little blue box). Waxed thread is treated with beeswax or microcrystalline wax.

**Cull your beads.** Remove beads that are wider or skinnier than the average-size bead—using consistently sized beads results in uniform beadwork.

To **pass through** means to pass through a bead a second time, moving the needle (or wire) in the same direction as the first pass *(fig. 02)*.

To **pass back through,** move the needle (or wire) in the opposite direction as the first pass *(fig. 03)*.

**Repeat.** When the word *repeat* appears after a semicolon, repeat the instructions that precede it in that sentence only. For example, here you'll work the entire sequence three times for a grand total of 6 stitches and 3A: "Work 2 stitches with 1A in each stitch; repeat this sequence twice."

**Repeat from *.** Repeat the instructions, starting at the text that immediately follows the *.

**Repeat the thread path to reinforce.** Retrace the previous thread path to strengthen the row/round/loop *(fig. 04)*. You may need to weave through beads and work a turnaround before you are in position to retrace the thread path.

**Row vs round.** Rows of peyote stitch are worked back and forth; rounds are worked in a circle.

**Secure the thread and trim.** Tie 1 or 2 knots around threads between nearby beads, weave through 3 to 4 beads, and trim the tail close to the beadwork with scissors or a thread burner. (See Starting and Ending Threads on page 19 for more information on forming knots.)

**Splitting the pairs.** Work 1 bead between the 2 beads of a pair in the previous row/round *(fig. 05)*. See Increase Stitches on page 21 for more information.

**Step up.** Use a step up to prepare for the next row (or round). Unless otherwise directed, do this by passing through the first bead added in the current row/round. It's not uncommon to step up through 2 beads at a time.

When directed to **work a stitch,** string 1 bead and pass through the next bead (or if bead-embroidering, pass down through the beading foundation). The motion of stringing the bead you want to add and going through the next to lock the bead in place is considered 1 stitch.

**String 1A (or 1B, 1C, etc.).** Use a needle to pick up one of the beads designated A (or B, C, etc.) in the materials list and slide it onto the thread.

**String {1A, 2B, and 2A} four times.** Repeat the entire sequence inside of the brackets four times. In this example, the strand would begin with 1A, 2B, 2A, 1A, 2B, 2A, etc. (not 4A, 8B, 8A).

**Turnaround.** Change the direction of beading without exposing the thread or deviating from the established thread path. See how-tos on page 23.

**Up bead vs down bead.** The top jagged end of a flat strip of peyote consists of up beads; the bottom end is made of down beads. In circular peyote stitch, up beads make up the outside edge; down beads are on the inside of the circle. In tubular peyote stitch, up beads are along the top of the tube; down beads are on the bottom of the tube. The very basic nature of peyote is to string 1 bead and pass through the nearest up bead. The bead just added becomes the new up bead; the bead just passed through is now a down bead.

**Weave through beads.** Pass your needle through beads until you exit the bead indicated in the pattern. Take the path that leaves no exposed threads and don't make any moves that might tweak the beadwork by pulling a bead in an undesired direction *(fig. 06)*.

**Working thread.** The working thread is the end with the needle, doing the work of stitching. The opposite end is the **tail thread.**

## BEADING + PEYOTE 101
### stringing
When stringing, simply use a needle and thread or wire (beading or gauged) to pick up beads and gather them into a strand *(fig. 07)*.

### threading the needle
Instead of holding your needle out in front of you and passing the thread through the eye, think of "needling the thread." To do so, hold the thread between the thumb and index finger of your nondominant hand with the thread just barely sticking out, just ¹⁄₁₆" (.2 cm) or so. Use your other hand to slide the eye of the needle down over the tip of the thread *(fig. 08)*.

Slide the needle down the thread so about ⅓ of the thread folds back onto itself. As you work, move the needle down the length of the thread as needed to control the amount of working thread.

### starting and ending threads
When starting a new project, leave a 6" (15.2 cm) tail so you have something to hold onto when working the first few rounds or rows. Sometimes a project will call for you to leave a longer tail to use during a later step; don't trim until indicated.

Some beaders like to add a **stop bead** in a contrasting color before the first beads strung. This bead prevents beads from sliding off the thread. Although a stop bead is also sometimes called a "tension bead," it usually slides around too much to offer any tension control. To lessen its tendency to slide around, pass through the stop bead twice; avoid splitting the thread of the first pass. Be sure to remove the stop bead before completing your project *(fig. 09)*.

To **end a thread,** make an overhand knot over a previous thread: Exit the bead closest to where you want the knot, pass the needle under the nearest thread of a previous row (or round) from back to front. Pull the thread to form a ¼" (.6 cm) loop and pass through the loop from back to front *(fig. 10)*. Pull to secure the knot. Weave through a few more beads before trimming. If desired, tie a second knot and weave through more beads before trimming for extra security. Never trim the thread next to the knot—it will always find a way to come undone.

To **add more thread midproject,** pass the needle with the new thread under a previous thread a few stitches away from where you want to resume beading, leaving a 4" (10.2 cm) tail. Tie 2 overhand knots around the previous thread and weave through beads to pick up where you left off. Add a needle to the new thread's tail and weave it through beads before trimming the thread *(fig. 11,* new thread in red; old thread in blue). If you know it will be hard to tell where you left off (such as when working a spiral tubular rope), consider adding the new thread before ending the old thread. To hide any knot, tug the thread to pull the knot inside of a bead. However, only do this if you know you won't need to pass through the bead again later.

To avoid having to later thread a needle on the tail, try this trick: Pass the new thread through a few beads, tie a half-hitch knot around a previous thread, and weave through a few more beads until you reach the bead you want to exit. Then, pull back on the tail thread to remove any slack and trim.

### single thread vs doubled thread
Unless otherwise directed, work your project using a single thread. If you are

using a durable thread and seed beads without sharp holes, a single thread is usually sufficient.

Using a **doubled thread** is great when working with large-holed beads. Using more thread fills the bead holes more quickly, and beads that have more thread hold tighter tension because they don't slide around as much. Doubled thread is also nice when working with crystals because the second thread adds a sense of security in the event a sharp crystal edge cuts a thread. Doubled thread is also great in sections of beadwork that benefit from reinforcement—such as when zipping the outermost rounds of a beaded ring or forming a loop of beads that connects a clasp.

To **double the thread** at the start of a project, begin with a thread that is twice as long as what you are used to working with, slide your needle to the center, and join the ends to double the thread.

Or, try this great method I picked up from Cynthia Rutledge: Start with a thread that is twice as long as what you are used to working with, work a few stitches, and then slide the needle toward the starting end of the thread so the tail extends a few inches beyond the last bead added. The thread is now doubled. This method is ideal when you want to double a thread midproject *(fig. 12)*.

Regardless of how you doubled the thread, you may have to slide your needle back to the center of the thread several times during the course of a project. If you need to undo any incorrect stitches, you may need to cut the fold and remove the needle.

### tangles and knots

To help **avoid pesky tangles,** keep your thread waxed or conditioned. If you notice your thread starting to twist, hold up the beadwork and allow the needle and thread to dangle and untwist. Stretching nylon thread after waxing/conditioning it can sometimes help avoid tangles. If a thread just won't stop tangling, end that thread and start a

new one; the first may just be too worn, or static may be causing the problem. Treat knots as you would tangles—wax/condition your thread as a preventative measure, and if all else fails, end that thread and start a new one. Once you see a knot start to form, use the tip of your needle to try to undo it before it gets too tight.

### correcting errors

**If you make an error,** fix it. You may be discouraged once you find a mistake, but you'll be much happier in the long run if you go back to correct it. Make light of the situation by thinking of it as the "frog stitch"—Rip it! Rip it!

When dealing with an **incorrect bead count,** it's often easy to remove an extra bead. Instead of tearing out the beadwork until you reach the misplaced bead (size 10° or smaller), carefully break it using the tip of chain-nose pliers. To do so, use the pliers to grip the bead you want to break, hold the piece down and away from you, and squeeze hard to break the bead. It's best to do this outside while wearing safety glasses. Beware that the process of breaking the bead may cut or damage your thread. Plus, the stitch that once held the bead may be loose; stitch back through beads to lessen the slack and reinforce the stitch. If you accidentally forgot a bead, it's best to rip out what you've done to correct the problematic stitch.

If you have a **broken bead,** first make sure that all small parts of the broken bead have been removed. You have two choices: 1) rip out what you've done and replace the broken bead with a new one, or 2) stitch a new bead in the empty spot created by the broken bead. If choosing the latter, be sure to repeat all of the thread paths around the new bead and use tight tension to pull the new bead down in place over the exposed thread left by the broken bead. The first option will give you the cleanest result but, if a bead breaks in a spot that would be extremely difficult to

undo, you can get away with the second option. For places where it's difficult to repeat the peyote thread path, you can square-stitch a new bead to the surrounding beads as long as your thread doesn't show too much *(fig. 13)*.

### tension

Tension describes the tightness of the thread as it passes through beads. Beadwork worked with tight tension will be stiff and rigid; beadwork worked with loose tension will be flexible. Tight tension is essential when making dimensional pieces.

To achieve **tight tension,** give the thread a strong tug after each stitch. It's natural for previously placed stitches to loosen as you work across a row (or round), so give the thread an extra pull at the end of each row or round before starting the next. Waxed or conditioned thread will be slightly sticky and will help set tension. You can also set tension by tying an inconspicuous knot.

If several rows are loose and need tightening, pull the beads and thread at the ends of previous rows and then pull the end of the working thread to continue removing unwanted slack *(fig. 14)*.

Sometimes **looser tension** is needed, but never use tension so loose that thread is left exposed between beads or so loose that a bead hangs from the beadwork. Think of it as relaxed tension—don't give the thread a hard tug after working each stitch. If a finished piece of beadwork is too rigid, a slight squeeze can break beads.

I naturally bead with tight tension, so when a lighter tension is needed, I consciously think of relaxing my hands. If you also use tight tension, try this trick I learned from Laura McCabe: Leave 1 or 2 bead's width of space when tying the starting ring of beads in a tubular or circular peyote-stitch project.

### peyote mantra

If you are new to peyote stitch, this is really the only thing you need to learn!

Think **"string 1 bead, skip 1 bead, and pass through the next"** as you stitch, and you'll see this mantra is the basic foundation of all peyote stitches.

## holding your work and first stitches

Some find the first 2 to 4 rows/rounds of peyote to be the hardest because the classic up and down pattern doesn't emerge until you've stitched a few rows/rounds. If this is your first time with peyote stitch, you may find it helpful to use large beads and a stiffer thread (such as FireLine) instead of nylon thread. Starting strips worked with nylon thread tend to be flexible and harder to hold. Wax your thread to keep the beads from sliding around.

To get started, string an even number of beads, alternating colors if desired. Working with your nondominant hand, use your thumb to hold this strand draped over the top of your index finger **(fig. 15)**. The needle and working thread will come toward you. Many like to work with a long tail wrapped around their pinky or several fingers—find what is most comfortable for you.

Now you are ready for the peyote mantra, "String 1 bead, skip 1 bead, and pass through the next." Don't worry if all of the beads are loose **(fig. 16)**. After working the row, pull the tail and working threads, and pinch and slide the beads down as needed to remove all slack in the thread and to encourage the beads to stack (some beads become up beads and others become down beads) **(fig. 17)**.

## two-drop peyote stitch

Instead of working just 1 bead in each stitch, work with 2 beads. When working subsequent rows/rounds, treat the 2 beads as 1 unless otherwise indicated **(fig. 18)**.

## increase stitches

Grow the size of the work by making increases. To do so, add 2 beads where you would have usually added just 1. If working with seed beads, choose 2

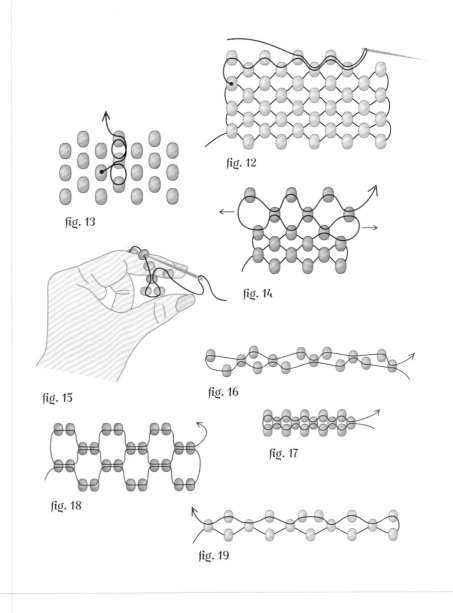

fig. 12

fig. 13

fig. 14

fig. 15

fig. 16

fig. 17

fig. 18

fig. 19

beads that are a little skinnier than the rest to make the increase more gradual **(fig. 19)**.

When working the next row/round, peyote-stitch 1 bead between each bead of the previous row, including the 2 beads worked for the increase. This is known as "splitting the pair." Again, for a gradual increase, choose a narrow bead. Notice the flat peyote-stitch sample shown here started 10 beads

wide and is now 12 beads wide. For tips on counting rows, see page 27; for rounds, see page 47 **(fig. 20)**.

Here's a nice way to work a more gradual increase featured in Jeannette Cook and Vicki Star's *Beading with Peyote Stitch* (Interweave, 2000): Work the row/round after the increase with 1 bead in each stitch, treating the increase pair of the previous row/round as 1 bead (green thread). When working the

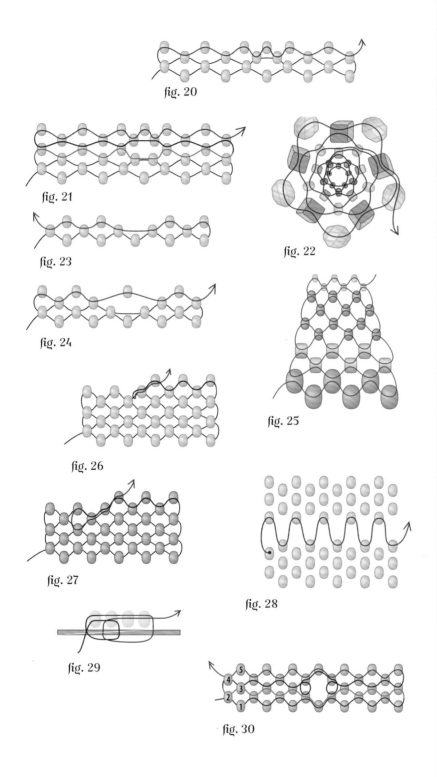

fig. 20

fig. 21

fig. 23

fig. 22

fig. 24

fig. 25

fig. 26

fig. 27

fig. 28

fig. 29

fig. 30

next row/round, add 2 beads above the increase stitch **(blue thread)**. Then, in the following row/round, work the more dramatic increase with 1 bead in each stitch, splitting the pair of the previous row/round **(fig. 21, red)**.

Instead of varying the number of beads to achieve an increase, work each row/round with progressively larger beads **(fig. 22)**.

To work increases along the edge of a flat peyote strip, see page 30. For more information on increasing circular peyote stitch, see page 48. For tubular peyote-stitch increases, see page 70.

## decrease stitches

To decrease the width of the beadwork mid-row/round, work the stitch where you want the decrease to start as usual, but don't add a bead. Instead, pass from 1 up bead of the previous row/round to the next **(fig. 23)**.

Peyote-stitch the following row/round as usual, adding 1 bead in each stitch. To make the decrease more gradual, choose a wider bead when stitching over the decrease. Notice the flat peyote-stitch sample shown here started 10 beads wide and is now 8 beads wide **(fig. 24)**.

Instead of varying the number of beads to achieve a decrease, work each row/round with progressively smaller beads **(fig. 25)**.

To work decreases at the end of a flat peyote row, see page 30. For more information on decreasing circular peyote stitch, see page 49. For tubular peyote-stitch decreases, see page 70.

## turnarounds

To exit a bead in the opposite direction, or to reverse the general direction of stitching, work a turnaround by looping your needle around thread(s) of previous rows/rounds and passing back through the last bead(s) exited **(fig. 26)**.

Or, weave through beads to change direction, making two 90° turns by passing through 2 beads in the same column **(fig. 27)**.

## zipping

Two edges of peyote stitch can be "zipped" together by passing from the up bead on one side of the beadwork to the up bead on the other side of the beadwork, interlocking the beads like teeth on a zipper. If using this method to turn a flat strip of peyote into a tube, make sure the strip is worked with an even number of rows **(fig. 28)**.

## backstitch bead embroidery

It's easy to work peyote stitch off a fabric or other foundation by attaching the first set of beads with backstitch. To begin, pass through the foundation from back to front. String 2 beads and slide them down to the backing. Pass down through the foundation next to the last bead added. Pass up through the foundation before the first bead added, then pass through the first and second beads **(fig. 29, blue)**. String 2 beads, pass down through the foundation next to the last bead strung, pass up between the first and second beads, then pass through the last 3 beads **(fig. 29, red)**; repeat. If working peyote stitch off this set of beads, these become the beads of both Rows/Rounds 1 and 2.

## small openings

Use the aid of square stitches when leaving small holes in the body of the work. Learn the technique by following this sample in flat peyote stitch and apply it to other peyote variations in the same manner.

**ROWS 1 AND 2** String 14 beads **(fig. 30, purple)**.

**ROW 3** String 1 bead, skip 1 bead previously strung, and pass through the next bead; repeat twice. Pass through the next bead of Row 1 and the next bead of Row 2 to form a decrease. String 1 bead, skip 1 bead previously strung, and pass through

the next bead; repeat twice **(fig. 30, green)**.

**ROW 4** Work 3 peyote stitches with 1 bead in each stitch. String 1 bead and square-stitch it to the nearest bead of Row 2. String 2 beads. Square-stitch the last bead just added to the next bead of Row 2 and pass through the next bead of Row 3. Work 2 peyote stitches with 1 bead in each stitch **(fig. 30, blue)**.

**ROW 5** Work 3 peyote stitches with 1 bead in each stitch. Pass through the next bead added in Row 4 (the bead strung between the square stitches) and the next bead of Row 4. Work 3 peyote stitches with 1 bead in each stitch to finish the row **(fig. 30, red)**.

**ROWS 6 AND ON** Continue working in peyote stitch as usual.

## large openings

To create a large opening, work different sections of peyote and then join the parts, leaving a hole in the center. Learn the technique by following this sample in flat peyote stitch and apply it to other peyote variations in the same manner.

**ROWS 1 AND 2** String 14 beads.

**ROW 3** String 1 bead, skip 1 bead previously strung, and pass through the next; repeat six times to add a total of 7 beads **(fig. 31, black)**.

**ROWS 4–8, LEFT STRIP** Work 2 peyote stitches with 1 bead in each stitch in each of 5 rows **(fig. 31, green)**. Weave through beads to exit the third bead of Row 3 **(fig. 31, blue)**.

**ROWS 4–8, RIGHT STRIP** Work 2 peyote stitches with 1 bead in each stitch in each of 5 rows **(fig. 31, red)**.

**ROW 9** Work 2 peyote stitches with 1 bead in each stitch. String 6 beads to bridge the gap over the 6 beads skipped in Rows 1–3. String another bead (the first bead of the left column) and pass through the next bead of Row 8, left strip. Work 1 peyote stitch with 1 bead **(fig. 32, blue)**.

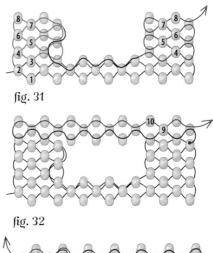

fig. 31

fig. 32

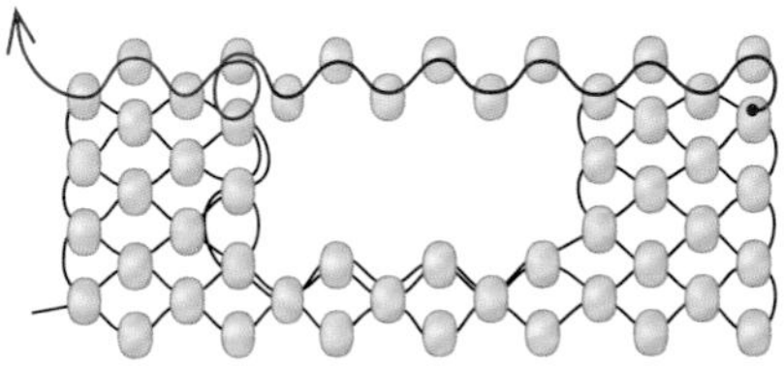

fig. 33

**ROWS 10 AND ON** Resume peyote stitch as usual **(fig. 32, red)**.

*Note:* If the first bead added for the left strip in Row 9 doesn't feel secure, square-stitch it to the nearest bead of the same column before continuing across the row in peyote **(fig. 33)**.

Alternatively, you can work the bottom, one side, and the top of an opening **(fig. 34)**. To close the opening, work the remaining side from the bottom up to meet the top strip **(fig. 35)**.

## accent bead insertions

Instead of leaving an opening in the beadwork, fill the hole with a larger accent bead. Learn the technique by following this sample in flat peyote stitch and apply it to other peyote variations in the same manner.

**ROWS 1 AND 2** String 14 seed beads **(fig. 36, brown)**.

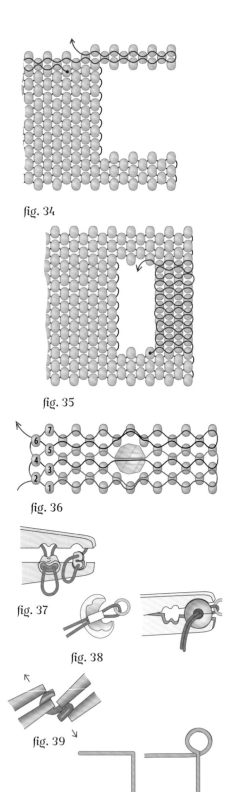

fig. 34

fig. 35

fig. 36

fig. 37

fig. 38

fig. 39

fig. 40    fig. 41

**ROW 3** String 1 seed bead, skip 1 bead previously strung, and pass through the next bead; repeat twice. Pass through the next bead of Row 1 and the next bead of Row 2 to form a decrease. String 1 seed bead, skip 1 bead previously strung, and pass through the next bead; repeat twice **(fig. 36, orange)**.

**ROW 4** Work 3 peyote stitches with 1 seed bead in each stitch. String the accent bead and pass through the next bead of Row 3. Work 2 peyote stitches with 1 seed bead in each stitch **(fig. 36, purple)**.

**ROW 5** Work 2 peyote stitches with 1 seed bead in each stitch. String 1 seed bead; pass through the ac- cent bead. Work 3 peyote stitches with 1 seed bead in each stitch **(fig. 36, green)**.

**ROW 6** Work 3 peyote stitches with 1 seed bead in each stitch. String 3 seed beads and pass through the next bead of Row 5. Work 2 peyote stitches with 1 seed bead in each stitch **(fig. 36, blue)**.

**ROW 7** Work 3 peyote stitches with 1 seed bead in each stitch. Pass through the next 2 beads of Row 6. Work 3 peyote stitches with 1 seed bead in each stitch **(fig. 36, red)**.

**ROWS 8 AND ON** Continue working in peyote stitch as usual.

### tight spots

Don't get discouraged if you find your- self in a tough situation where you just can't angle the needle exactly where you want it to go. For example, if you work a bezeled rivoli with tight tension and later want to add embellishments, the work might be too tight to offer any give when trying to angle your needle. In this situation, the needle may want to pass through more than just the one bead you intended. Go ahead and make the stitch, then simply remove the needle and pull the thread back out of the bead(s) you didn't intend to pass through.

## CRIMPING, WIREWORKING + KNOTTING

### crimping

This is a technique by which you mold a crimp tube around beading wire using crimping or flat-nose pliers.

**Crimp tubes:** Use beading wire to string 1 crimp tube, pass through a finding, and pass back through the tube, leaving a ¼" to ½" (.6 to 1.3 cm) tail. Make sure the wires do not cross inside the tube. Pinch the tube into a U shape, using the back notch of the crimping pli- ers. Each wire should now be contained in its own chamber. Turn the pinched tube 90° and use the front notch of the crimping pliers to fold it into a cylinder. Trim the excess wire **(fig. 37)**.

**Crimp covers:** Hold the cover in the front notch of the crimping pliers, posi- tion it over a crimped crimp tube, and gently squeeze the pliers to form the C-shaped finding into a round bead. For a perfectly round crimp cover, rotate the pliers around the cover just before you pinch the cover completely closed **(fig. 38)**.

### basic wirework

**Jump rings:** Using 2 pairs of chain- or flat-nose pliers (round-nose pliers usually leave marks) or a combination of the two, open and close a jump ring by twisting the sides in opposite directions, one side straight toward you and one side straight away from you (pulling the ends away from each other will distort the rings). To close the jump ring, reverse this action **(fig. 39)**.

A **simple loop** can be opened and closed like a jump ring, so if you want to change its placement, you can do so easily. Because there is a small open- ing in the loop, beware that a beading thread could slip through.

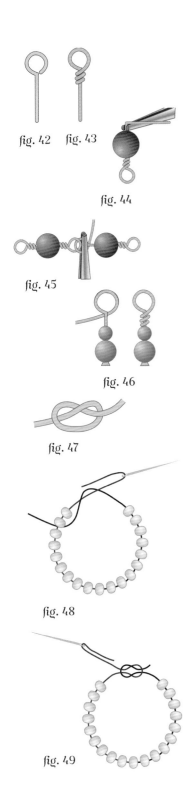

fig. 42    fig. 43

fig. 44

fig. 45

fig. 46

fig. 47

fig. 48

fig. 49

Use chain- or flat-nose pliers to form a 90° bend ½" to 1" (1.3 to 2.5 cm) from the end of your wire *(fig. 40)*. Imagine the size of the loop you would like to make, then place the nose of the round-nose pliers on the short wire at a distance from the bend that equals about half of the circumference of the loop you imagined. Roll the pliers toward the bend, then use your finger to wrap the short wire the rest of the way round the pliers, adjusting the pliers as needed, until the short wire crosses the bend at the base of the loop *(fig. 41)*.

While still holding the loop in the pliers, adjust the wire below the bend as needed to restore the 90° angle. Trim the wire next to the bend *(fig. 42)*.

A **wrapped loop** is a sturdy loop that is preferable when creating a dangle or link that is heavy or will incur strain. Because it can't open like a simple loop once complete, it's safe to attach beading thread to this type of loop. To begin, use chain- or flat-nose pliers to form a 90° bend 1" to 2" (2.5 to 5.1 cm) from the end of your wire.

Make a simple loop, but don't trim the tail. Grasp the loop with chain-nose pliers. Using your fingers, or holding the end of the wire with chain- or flat-nose pliers, wrap the tail down the neck of the main wire at the base of the loop for about 2 or 3 wraps. Trim the wire at the end of the last wrap. For tight wraps, think of pulling the wire away from the loop as you wrap.

Once you've trimmed the wire after making wraps, press the cut end down with either flat-nose pliers or the front notch of crimping pliers *(fig. 43)*.

**Wrapped-loop link:** This is a piece of wire with wrapped loops on each end for attaching to other loops, chains, clasps, etc. Form a wrapped loop at one end of the wire and string a bead. Snug the bead down to the first loop and grasp the wire just above the bead using the tip of your chain-nose pliers. Make a 90° bend *(fig. 44)*.

Continue making a basic wrapped loop as before, but before wrapping the tail down the neck of the main wire, string a chain link, clasp, or other finding.

Grasp the loop just formed with the tip of the chain-nose pliers, holding the strung finding out of the way, and wrap the tail down the neck of the main wire. Trim to complete the wrapped loop *(fig. 45)*.

**Wrapped-loop dangle:** Use a head pin to string 1 or more beads and form a wrapped loop *(fig. 46)*.

## knotting

An **overhand knot** is the most basic knot. Make a loop with your stringing material by crossing the left end over the right. Pass the left end through the loop from the back so that it resembles a pretzel. Pull the thread tight *(fig. 47)*.

Use a **square knot** when securing the starting circle of beads for circular and tubular peyote stitch. Begin by tying an overhand knot: Cross the working thread *(fig. 48, red)* over the tail thread *(fig. 48, blue)* and pass the tail thread through the loop from front to back. Make a second overhand knot, passing the tail thread *(fig. 49, blue)* behind the working thread *(fig. 49, red)* and through the loop just formed from front to back. Pull the threads tight, making sure the knot is between the first and last beads of the circle. Before beginning the next round, pass the working thread through the first or last bead strung to correctly orient the thread, but don't pull so tight that the knot gets pulled inside the bead. If the knot slips inside the bead and fills the hole with thread, you'll have less room for your needle on subsequent passes. Forcing your needle through small spaces can cause bead breakage.

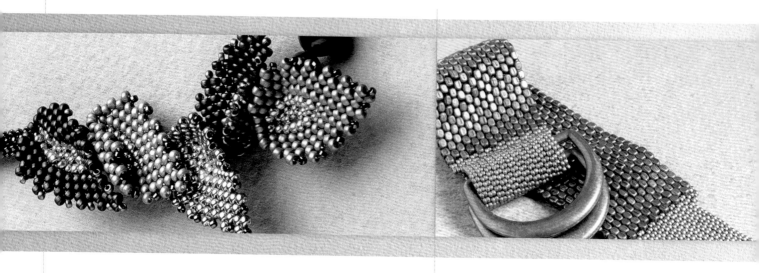

# flat peyote

Master flat peyote stitch and you'll quickly see it's the building block for all other peyote variations. But don't be fooled by its name—pieces made with this basic stitch can be curled, twisted, folded, and gathered to be anything but flat.

For a modern accessory made in irresistible matte-finished beads, start with Carole Ohl's **Buckle-Up Cuff.** Her use of triangle beads and two-drop flat peyote makes the bands quicker to stitch than you might initially think. Weave the fabric of beads through metal findings for a beltlike look.

The leaves in my **Walkin' After Midnight** necklace are a lesson in shaping with flat peyote stitch. By working both end-row increases and decreases, seemingly plain pieces of beadwork take on a leaf silhouette. Each leaf is gathered down the center to show how flat peyote need not be just two-dimensional.

*Perfect your flat peyote–stitch skills and you'll be ready to bead any peyote project you can dream up.*

## TECHNIQUES

### counting

When counting the number of rows in a piece of flat peyote stitch, don't simply count the beads along one edge. Instead, count the beads on the diagonal *(fig. 01)*.

Or, you can count in a zigzag pattern *(fig. 02)*.

When determining the total width, count each column of beads, not just the number of beads stitched in a single row *(fig. 03)*.

### even-count flat peyote stitch

Working in even-count peyote stitch is fast since no turnarounds are required.

Start by stringing an even number of beads. The first set of beads strung always makes up both Rows 1 *and* 2. Note the first bead strung becomes the first bead of Row 2, not Row 1 *(fig. 04)*.

To start the third row, string 1 bead, skip the last bead previously strung, and pass through the next. The first bead of Row 3 will sit on top of the last bead of Row 1 *(fig. 05)*.

Work across the row with 1 bead in each stitch following the peyote mantra: "String 1 bead, skip 1 bead, and pass through the next" *(fig. 06)*.

Work the fourth and following row(s) just as you worked Row 3. This example is 10 beads/columns wide (with 5 beads stitched in each row) and 5 rows long (or tall) *(fig. 07)*.

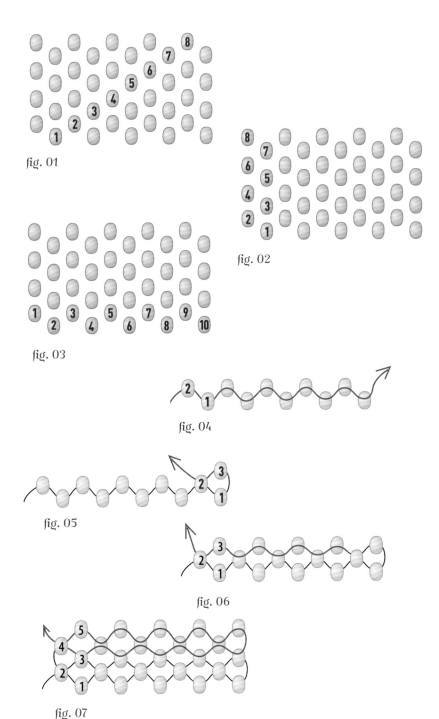

fig. 01

fig. 02

fig. 03

fig. 04

fig. 05

fig. 06

fig. 07

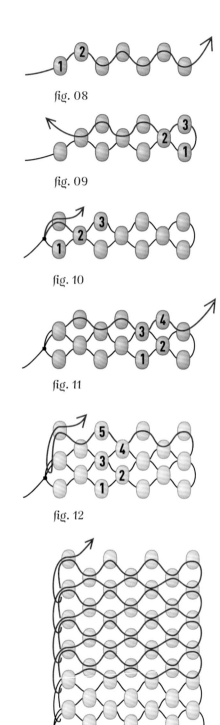

fig. 08

fig. 09

fig. 10

fig. 11

fig. 12

fig. 13

## odd-count flat peyote stitch

Working a strip of peyote with an odd number of beads is a great choice when creating a motif that needs to come to a point or if you intend to attach something to the very center bead of the beadwork. Here you'll see there are several ways to work turnarounds at the end of the odd-number rows.

Start by stringing an odd number of beads. As with even count, the first set of beads strung makes up both Rows 1 *and* 2. Note the first bead strung remains the first bead of Row 1 *(fig. 08)*.

For Row 3, string 1 bead, skip the last bead previously added, and pass through the next. Repeat until you exit the first bead of Row 2. Notice this row is worked just like even-count flat peyote *(fig. 09)*.

To finish Row 3, string 1 bead and tie a square knot with the tail and working threads. Pass back through the last bead strung to step up for the next row *(fig. 10)*.

For Row 4 and the following even-number rows, work across the row with 1 bead in each stitch *(fig. 11)*.

For Row 5 and the following odd-number rows, work across the row with 1 bead in each stitch until you exit the first bead of the previous row. Add the final bead of the row using one of the following methods:

### traditional turnaround
String 1 bead and pass the needle under the nearest thread loop at the end of the beadwork. Pass back through the last bead strung to step up for the next row. This is the most common way of working an odd-count turnaround *(fig. 12)*.

Alternate Rows 4 and 5 for the length of the work. The left edge of the beadwork will have odd-count turnarounds; the right edge will resemble even-count peyote *(fig. 13)*.

### square-stitch add-on
Alternatively, you can finish odd-number rows with a square stitch: Before stringing the last bead of Row 3, pass back through the first bead of Row 1. String 1 bead, pass back through the first bead of Row 1 again, and through the bead just strung to complete the square stitch *(fig. 14)*.

### clockwise figure-eight add-on
Another way to add the last bead and step up for the next row is to work a figure-eight thread path in a clockwise direction: Before stringing the final bead of Row 3, pass back through the first bead of Row 1. String 1 bead, then pass back through the last bead exited in Row 2 and the next bead of Row 3 *(fig. 15, blue)*. Turn around by passing back through the second bead of Row 1, the next bead of Row 2, and the first bead of Row 1. Pass through the bead just added *(fig. 15, red)*.

### counterclockwise figure-eight add-on

Or, add the last bead with a counter-clockwise figure-eight thread path: String 1 bead, pass through the first bead of Row 1, the nearest bead of Row 2, and the next bead of Row 1 *(fig. 16, blue)*. Turn around by passing through the second-to-last bead of Row 3, back through the nearest bead of Row 2, and back through the first bead of Row 1. Pass through the bead just added *(fig. 16, red)*.

## two-needle peyote stitch

By working two-needle peyote stitch you avoid the need to work any of the turnarounds just described. Also, you can avoid the extra thread bulk that typically builds up on one side of an odd-count strip.

To begin, add a needle to each end of a comfortable length of thread and string an odd number of beads. Slide the beads to the center of the thread. This first set of beads makes up both Rows 1 and 2.

For Row 3, use the right needle to work across the row with 1 bead in each stitch. String 1 more bead. Set the needle down *(fig. 17, blue)*. Use the left needle to pass back through the last bead added *(fig. 17, red)*.

Work 2 rows with 1 bead in each stitch. String 1 more bead. Set the needle down *(fig. 18, red)*. Use the other needle to pass back through the last bead added *(fig. 18, blue)*.

Continue working in the same manner, stitching 2 rows with 1 needle before switching to the other needle *(fig. 19)*.

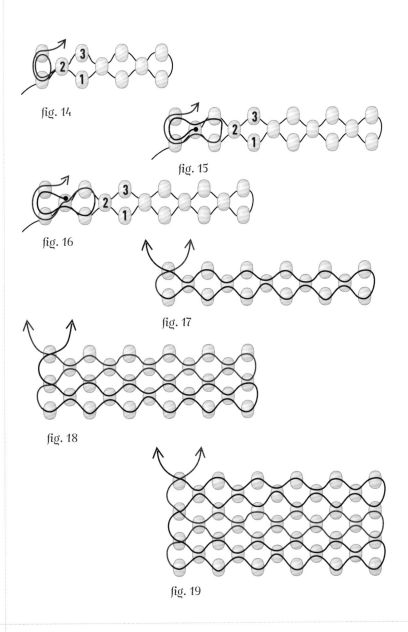

fig. 14

fig. 15

fig. 16

fig. 17

fig. 18

fig. 19

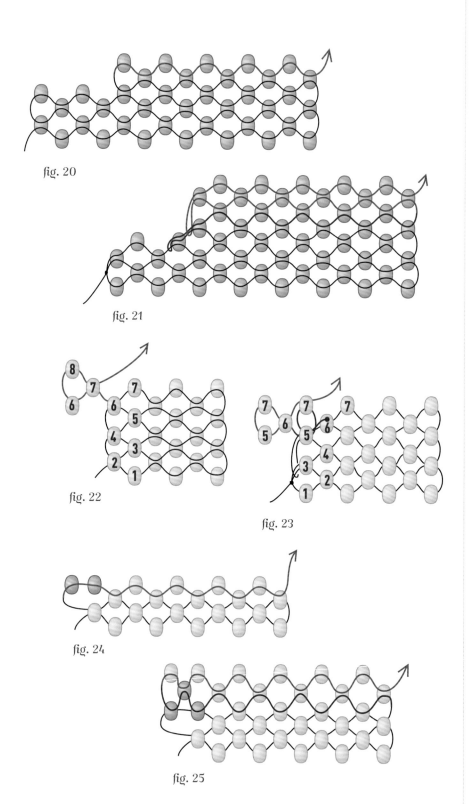

fig. 20

fig. 21

fig. 22

fig. 23

fig. 24

fig. 25

## end-row decrease

Regardless if your starting rows contain an odd or even number of beads, there are two ways to work an end-row decrease. Choose the one that achieves the result you want.

The first way is to simply stop the row a few beads short and start working the following row as usual **(fig. 20)**.

In the second method, work a turnaround by looping the thread around the previous row's thread. To do so, string the last bead of the row, pass through the next bead, work the turnaround loop, and pass back through the last 2 beads **(fig. 21, blue)**. Or, work a traditional odd-count turnaround: String the last bead of the row, work the turnaround loop, and pass back through the last bead added **(fig. 21, red)**.

## end-row increase

Add columns of beads at the side of a peyote strip for a large, stair-stepped increase. Or, gradually grow the width of the beadwork by increasing the number of beads used in the edge stitches.

### increasing even-count peyote

To work an increase at the side of a piece of even-count peyote, string 3 beads before starting the next row. Pass back through the first of these 3 beads. Note the first bead of the set is part of the row just worked (Row 7 in **fig. 22**), the second bead strung is part of the previous row (Row 6), and the third bead is the first bead of the newest row (Row 8) **(fig. 22)**.

### increasing odd-count peyote

To work an increase at the side of a piece of odd-count peyote (the side with the thread-loop turnarounds), work across the final row as usual. Attach the final bead of the row with a square stitch *(fig. 23, blue)*. String 3 beads. Pass back through the first of these 3 and the square-stitched bead *(fig. 23, red)*.

### gradual increase

For a smoother, more gradual increase, work increase stitches along the side of a flat peyote strip: After exiting the end of a row, string 2 beads for the first stitch of the following row. Work across the row as usual *(fig. 24)*.

Peyote-stitch across the row with 1 bead in each stitch, splitting the pair of increase beads at the end of the row *(fig. 25, blue)*. Stitch the following row as usual *(fig. 25, red)*.

For a dramatic increase, work increase stitches in every stitch on the left side of the work. For a subtler increase, work a few rows with just 1 bead in each stitch before adding increase beads again. To cause the beadwork to fan out in both directions, work increase stitches on both sides of the strip.

## diagonal peyote stitch

This fun variation on peyote stitch uses end-row increases and decreases to create a strip of beadwork that's somewhat a trick of the eye—at first glance it can be hard to tell projects worked with this stitch are peyote. See example on page 45. Learn the technique by following this sample; size 15's are used at

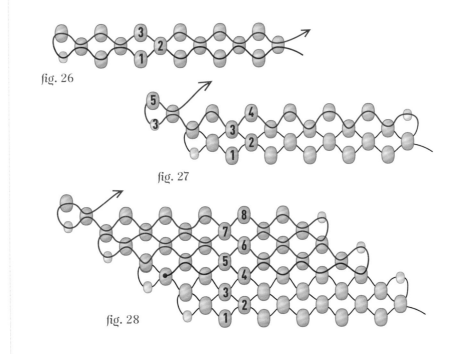

fig. 26

fig. 27

fig. 28

the ends for decorative purposes, but play around with your own bead combinations. Begin with an even number of beads:

**ROWS 1 AND 2** String 11 size 11's and 1 size 15° *(fig. 26, blue)*.

**ROW 3** String 1 size 11°, skip 1 bead previously strung, and pass through the next; repeat five times to add a total of 6 size 11's *(fig. 26, red)*.

**ROW 4** Work 1 stitch with 1 size 15°. Work 5 stitches with 1 size 11° in each stitch. To work an increase, string 1 size 11°, 1 size 15°, and 1 size 11°; pass back through the first size 11° just added. **note:** *The size 15° just added will become a down bead and part of the previous row; the second size 11° just added will become an up bead and part of the next row* *(fig. 27)*.

**ROW 5** Work 5 stitches with 1 size 11° in each stitch *(fig. 28, blue)*.

**ROWS 6 AND ON** Repeat Rows 4 and 5 for the length of the band *(fig. 28, red)*.

# buckle-up cuff

Carole loves to discover unusual clasps. She often shops in the notions section of sewing stores or in scrapbooking stores, to find items that might be used for a closure. In this case, the D-ring gives the look of a buckle clasp, but the true closure is a hidden hook-and-loop fastener. • *by carole ohl*

**TECHNIQUES**

Flat peyote stitch

Zipping

**MATERIALS**

7 g olive-gold matte metallic size 15° Japanese seed beads (A)

22 g total size 11° Japanese sharp triangles in olivine matte metallic iris, gold-lined crystal AB, and gold bronze matte metallic (B)

2 bronze 1½" × 1³/₁₆" (3.8 × 3 cm) D-rings

1 black ½" (1.3 cm) or ⅝" (1.6 cm) hook-and-loop adhesive dot set

Smoke 6 lb braided beading thread

**TOOLS**

Scissors

Size 11 beading needle

**FINISHED SIZE**

1½" × 7" (3.8 × 17.8 cm)

**NOTE**

*The instructions here are for the gold colorway. See page 35 for information on the gunmetal and blue colorway.*

**TIPS**

• This design works best using triangles with sharp edges. You'll notice that some triangles on the market are more bulbous with very round edges.

• When shopping for D-rings at your craft or sewing store, you'll see them among the findings made for purses and bags.

fig. 01: rows 1–3

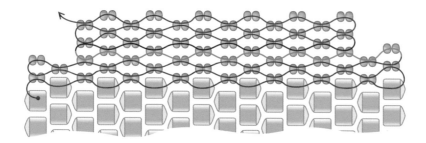

fig. 02: starting the D-ring connection band

fig. 03: zipping the D-ring connection band

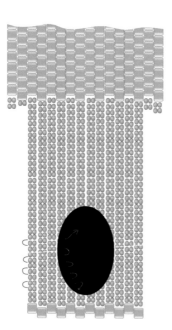

fig. 04: attaching the hook half of the dot

## 1 center band.

**1** **center band.** Work one-drop flat peyote stitch with triangle beads to form a wide band for the center of the cuff:

**ROWS 1 AND 2** Mix the B beads to form "bead soup" and use the colors at random. Use 6' (1.8 m) of thread to string 16B, leaving a 12" (30.5 cm) tail *(fig. 01, blue)*.

**ROW 3** String 1B, skip 1B previously strung, and pass through the next B; repeat to add a total of 8B *(fig. 01, red)*.

**ROWS 4–139** Work 1B in each stitch to add a total of 8B in each of 136 rows, or until you reach the desired length minus 1¾" (4.4 cm) for the closure. If adjusting the size, be sure you end with an odd number of total rows.

## 2 d-ring connection band.

**2** **d-ring connection band.** Use two-drop flat peyote stitch and size 15's to form a band that connects the D-rings to the center band:

**ROWS 1–3** Work 8 stitches with 2A in each stitch to add a total of 16A in each of 3 rows *(fig. 02, purple)*.

**ROW 4** Work 7 stitches with 2A in each stitch to add a total of 14A, stopping short before the end of the row *(fig. 02, green)*.

**ROW 5** Work 6 stitches with 2A in each stitch to add a total of 12A, stopping short before the end of the row *(fig. 02, blue)*.

**ROWS 6–55** Work 6 stitches with 2A in each stitch to add a total of 12A in each of 50 rows *(fig. 02, red)*.

**ZIP** Pass the end of the strip up through both D-rings. Fold the connection band down toward the last row of the center band. Zip Row 55 of the connection band to the final row of B at the end of the center band *(fig. 03)*. Secure the thread and trim; don't trim the tail.

**3 clasp band.** Use two-drop flat peyote stitch and size 15°s to form a band that closes the cuff:

**ROWS 1–5** Use the tail thread to repeat Step 2, Rows 1–5.

**ROWS 6–72** Work 6 stitches with 2A in each stitch to add a total of 12A in each of 67 rows, adding thread as needed.

**ROW 73** String 1B and pass through the next 2A of the previous row; repeat to add a total of 6B.

**ROW 74** Work 1B in each stitch to add a total of 6B. Secure the thread but don't trim it.

**4 clasp.** Press the hook half of 1 hook-and-loop dot on the front of the clasp band, positioning it so its center is about ⅝" (1.6 cm) from the end. **note:** *To determine the front of the bracelet, remember the zipped edge of the connection band is on the back.*

Weave through beads to exit under the dot. Pass up through the dot, take a ¹⁄₁₆" to ⅛" (.2 to .3 cm) long stitch, and pass back down through the dot to exit the back of the clasp band. Pass through a few beads of the clasp band to exit another spot under the dot and repeat stitching *(fig. 04)*. Continue stitching the dot in place until secure. Secure the thread and trim.

Press the loop half of the dot on the front of the center band, positioning it so its center is about ⅞" (2.2 cm) from the center band/ connection band dividing line. Use 8" (20.3 cm) of new thread to stitch the dot in place as before. Secure the thread and trim.

To wear, pass the end of the clasp band up through both D-rings from back to front, then pass down through the first D-ring (as when fastening a belt buckle), and press the hook-and-loop dots together.

**TIPS**

● When using triangles, let your own sense of design determine how you like the triangles to lie. If you like a more orderly, tidy look, alternate pointing up, then pointing down. If you prefer a more organic, artsy look, let them point in random directions.

● When beading with multiple colors, you can mix the beads before you start or keep them in piles of separate colors so you can more easily choose which color you want to use next. The latter is useful if you have a low quantity of a bead you want to use. This will help you ration the beads so they are evenly distributed in your design.

● If you're concerned that the hook-and-loop closure may wear out with heavy use, attach the adhesive dots with separate threads so you can easily replace them without affecting the beaded structure.

**DESIGN OPTIONS**

● To make the rich gunmetal and deep blue colorway (page 32), follow the instructions as for the mustard-colored cuff using the following materials: For A, use brown metallic iris size 15° Japanese seed beads. For B, use a mix of size 11° Japanese sharp triangles in brown metallic iris, jet black matte metallic iris, and sage gray matte metallic. Finish the cuff with gunmetal 1½" × 1³⁄₁₆" (3.8 × 3 cm) D-rings and 1 black ½" (1.3 cm) or ⅝" (1.6 cm) hook-and-loop adhesive dot set.

*Play with beads other than triangles for the center band. Here, Carole used metal 3×2mm cubes gleaned from a piece of vintage jewelry.*

Elegantly asymmetrical, this necklace showcases the versatility of flat peyote stitch. Work simple increases, decreases, and row-end embellishments to create the dimensional leaves and then stitch them to an armature of Ultrasuede and seed beads. The colors are inspired by the silvery hues of leaves in moonlight. ● *by melinda barta*

# walkin' after midnight

**TECHNIQUES**

Flat and tubular peyote stitch

Sewing

Stringing

**MATERIALS**

6 g plum hematite metallic size 15° Japanese seed beads (A)

1 g 24k gold electroplate size 15° Japanese seed beads (B)

1 g silvery green matte metallic iris size 15° Japanese seed beads (C)

7 g purple/copper matte metallic iris size 11° Japanese seed beads (D)

2 g gold Duracoat galvanized size 11° Japanese seed beads (E)

2 g silver sage matte permanent galvanized size 11° Japanese seed beads (F)

3 g dark steel/silver sage permanent galvanized size 11° Japanese seed beads (G)

2 g gray mist matte metallic size 11° Japanese seed beads (H)

2 blue matte metallic iris size 8° Japanese seed beads (I)

2 night blue 6mm crystal pearls

12 night blue 8mm crystal pearls

1 nickel-plated size 1 (7x12mm) hook-and-eye set

5 × 2" (12.7 × 5.1 cm) piece of burgundy Ultrasuede

Smoke 6 lb braided beading thread

Microcrystalline wax

**TOOLS**

Scissors

Size 10 and 12 beading needles

**FINISHED SIZE**

23¾" (57.8 cm)

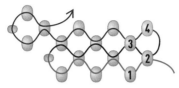

fig. 01: working rows
1–4 of the leaf

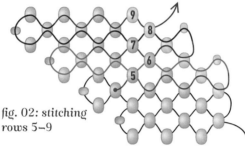

fig. 02: stitching
rows 5–9

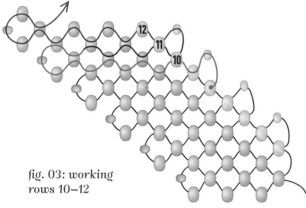

fig. 03: working
rows 10–12

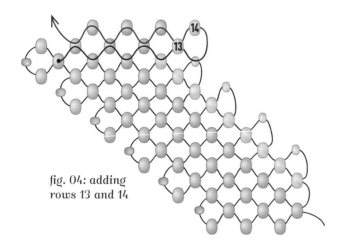

fig. 04: adding
rows 13 and 14

**1** **leaf body.** Use flat peyote stitch and a series of increases and decreases to create the body of the leaf. note: *Start with the size 10 needle and switch to the size 12 if you ever have trouble fitting the needle through beads.*

**ROWS 1 AND 2** Use 3' (.9 m) of waxed thread to string 6F and 1A, leaving a 6" (15.2 cm) tail *(fig. 01, green)*.

**ROW 3** String 1F, skip the last 2 beads previously strung, and pass through the next. String 1F, skip the next bead, and pass through the following; repeat to add a total of 3F *(fig. 01, blue)*.

**ROW 4** Work 1 stitch with 1E. Work 2 stitches with 1F in each stitch. To work an increase, string 2F, 1A, and 1F; pass back through the first F just added *(fig. 01, red)*. note: *The second F just added will become a down bead and part of the previous row; the third F just added will become an up bead and part of the next row.*

**ROW 5** Work 2 stitches with 1F in each stitch. Work 1 stitch with 1E *(fig. 02, pink)*.

**ROW 6** Work 1 stitch with 1B. Work 1 stitch with 1E. Work 2 stitches with 1F in each stitch. To work an increase, string 2F, 1A, and 1F; pass back through the first F just added *(fig. 02, green)*.

**ROW 7** Repeat Row 5 *(fig. 02, purple)*.

**ROW 8** Repeat Row 6 *(fig. 02, blue)*.

**ROW 9** Repeat Row 5 *(fig. 02, red)*.

**ROW 10** Repeat Row 6 *(fig. 03, green)*.

**ROW 11** Repeat Row 5 *(fig. 03, blue)*.

**ROW 12** Repeat Row 6 *(fig. 03, red)*.

**ROW 13** Work 3 stitches with 1F in each stitch. Work 1 stitch with 1E *(fig. 04, blue)*.

**ROW 14** Work 1 stitch with 1E. Work 3 stitches with 1F in each stitch *(fig. 04, red)*.

**ROW 15** String 1A and 1F; pass back through the last F of the previous row to form the first stitch of this row. Work 3 stitches with 1F in each stitch. To work an increase, string 1E, 1B, and 1E; pass back through the first E just added *(fig. 05, green thread)*.

**ROW 16** Work 3 stitches with 1F in each stitch *(fig. 05, blue thread)*.

**ROW 17** Repeat Row 15 *(fig. 05, red)*. note: *When adding the final F of this row (and Row 19), be sure to pass through the E added at the end of the Row 15 increase (as opposed to the B; the increase beads may accidentally twist, causing you to pass through the incorrect bead).*

**ROW 18** Repeat Row 16 *(fig. 06, maroon)*.

**ROW 19** Repeat Row 15 *(fig. 06, pink)*.

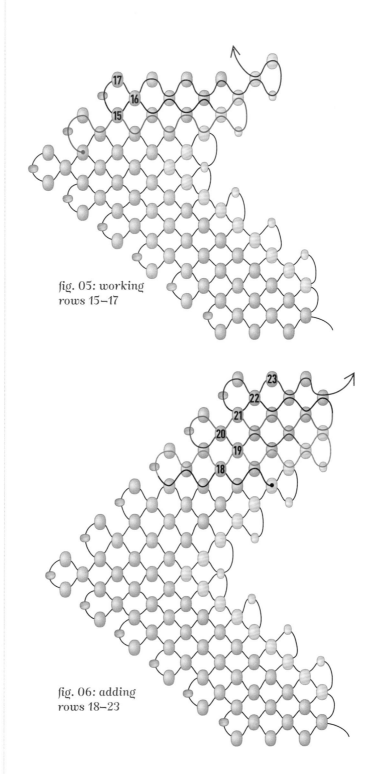

fig. 05: working rows 15–17

fig. 06: adding rows 18–23

**ROW 20** Repeat Row 16 *(fig. 06, purple)*.

**ROW 21** String 1A and 1F; pass back through the last F of the previous row to form the first stitch of this row. Work 3 stitches with 1F in each stitch *(fig. 06, green)*.

**ROW 22** Repeat Row 16 *(fig. 06, blue)*.

**ROW 23** String 1A and 1F; pass back through the last F of the previous row to form the first stitch of this row. Work 2 stitches with 1F in each stitch *(fig. 06, red)*. Secure the thread but don't trim.

**2 leaf shaping.** Join the beads along the centerline of the leaf to add dimension:

**CENTERLINE** Weave through beads to exit away from the beadwork from the B added at the end of the Row 19 increase. String 1B; pass through the B of Row 6 toward the beadwork. String 1B and pass through the next B on the bottom inside edge; repeat twice *(fig. 07, green)*. Weave through beads to exit the last B added in this step *(fig. 07, blue)*. Pass through the nearest B on the top inside edge and the second-to-last B added in this step. Pass through the next B on the top inside edge, the second B added in this step, and the B added at the end of the Row 19 increase *(fig. 07, red)*. note: *Use tight tension to pull the inside edges of the leaf toward the center and shape the beadwork. Repeat the thread path to reinforce. Don't trim the thread.*

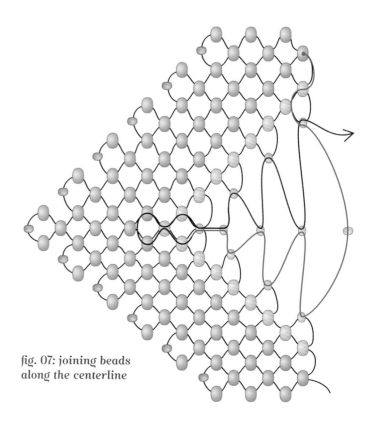

fig. 07: joining beads along the centerline

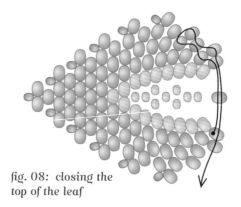

fig. 08: closing the top of the leaf

back of long base

**TOP** Add a needle to the tail thread. Fold the sides of the leaf toward each other. String 1F and pass through the first F of Row 22. Weave through beads to work a turnaround and repeat the thread path *(fig. 08)*. Secure the thread and trim. Fold the sides of the leaf back down away from each other but don't force the bead-work to flatten; instead, allow the gold center to remain folded. Repeat Steps 1 and 2 to make a second matte sage leaf. Repeat Steps 1 and 2 five times using C in place of A and D in place of F for a total of 5 purple/copper leaves. Repeat Steps 1 and 2 three times using G in place of F for a total of 3 dark steel/silver sage leaves. Repeat Steps 1 and 2 twice using H in place of F for a total of 2 gray mist leaves. Set the leaves aside.

**3** **short base.** Make a two-drop flat peyote–stitch strip and back it with Ultrasuede to form a base for the leaves on the left side of the necklace:

**ROWS 1 AND 2** Use 4' (1.2 m) of waxed thread to string 39D, 1I, and 2D *(fig. 09, blue)*.

**ROW 3** Skip the last 5 beads just added and pass back through the next 2D. String 2D, skip 2D previously strung, and pass back through the next 2D; repeat seven times to add a total of 16D. String 3D; pass through the first 3D added in this step *(fig. 09, red)*.

**ROW 4** Work 9 stitches off Row 3 with 2D in each stitch to add a total of 18D. Pass back through the 2D/I/2D at the end of the strip *(fig. 10, blue)*.

**ROW 5** Work 9 stitches off Row 2 with 2D in each stitch to add a total of 18D. Pass through the 6D at the top of the strip and exit the first 2D of Row 4 *(fig. 10, red)*.

**ROW 6** Work 8 stitches off Row 4 with 2D in each stitch to add a total of 16D. Pass through the 4D/I/4D at the end of the strip *(fig. 11, blue)*.

**ROW 7** Work 8 stitches off of Row 5 with 2A in each stitch to add a total of 16A. Pass through the

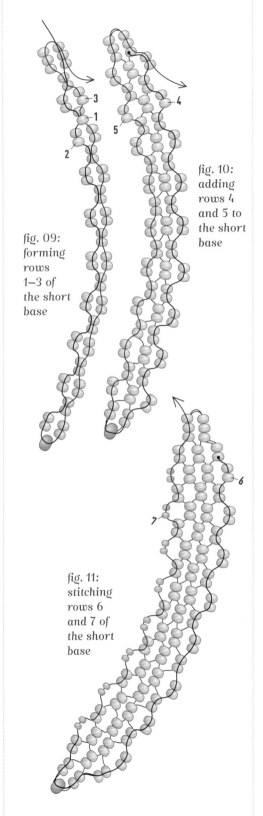

fig. 09: forming rows 1–3 of the short base

fig. 10: adding rows 4 and 5 to the short base

fig. 11: stitching rows 6 and 7 of the short base

41

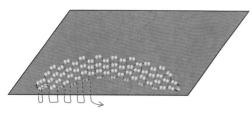

fig. 12: anchoring the short base to the Ultrasuede

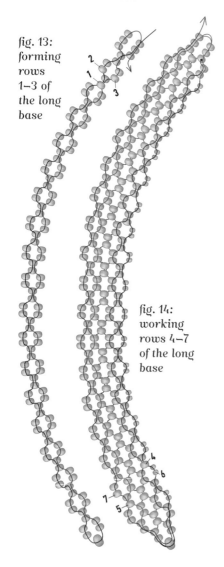

fig. 13: forming rows 1–3 of the long base

fig. 14: working rows 4–7 of the long base

nearest 3D at the top of the strip *(fig. 11, red)*. Use tight tension to cause the beadwork to curve but remain flat. Secure the thread to set the tension but don't trim.

**BACKING** Lay the strip of beadwork down on the piece of Ultrasuede near one edge to leave room for the large leaf base. Pass down through the Ultrasuede and back up to exit between the 2D last exited. Pass through the next 2 beads on the outside edge of the base, down through the Ultrasuede, and back up 2 beads away; repeat, sewing down the edge of the base and flattening the beadwork against the Ultrasuede as you work *(fig. 12)*. note: *Check to make sure the strip curves as shown in* **Fig. 11** *and that the work didn't accidentally flip.* Sew the 2D/I/2D at the end of the strip to the Ultrasuede in the same manner and continue stitching along the other side of the strip. Secure the thread and trim. Trim the Ultrasuede along the outside edge of the beadwork, taking care to avoid cutting stitches. Set the short base aside.

**4 long base.** Make a two-drop flat peyote–stitch strip and back it with Ultrasuede to form a base for the leaves on the right side of the necklace:

**ROWS 1 AND 2** Use 6' (1.8 m) of waxed thread to string 75D, 1I, and 2D *(fig. 13, blue)*.

**ROW 3** Skip the last 5 beads just added and pass back through the next 2D. String 2D, skip 2D previously strung, and pass back through the next 2D; repeat sixteen times to add a total of 34D. String 3D; pass through the first 3D added in this step *(fig. 13, red)*.

**ROW 4** Work 18 stitches off Row 3 with 2D in each stitch to add a total of 36D. Pass back through the 2D/I/2D at the end of the strip *(fig. 14, purple)*.

**ROW 5** Work 18 stitches off Row 2 with 2D in each stitch to add a total of 36D. Pass through the 6D at the top of the strip and exit the first 2D of Row 4 *(fig. 14, green)*.

**ROW 6** Work 17 stitches off Row 4 with 2A in each stitch to add a total of 34A. Pass through the 4D/I/4D at the end of the strip *(fig. 14, blue)*. Use tight tension to cause the beadwork to curve but remain flat.

**ROW 7** Work 17 stitches off Row 5 with 2D in each stitch to add a total of 34D. Pass through the nearest 3D at the top of the strip *(fig. 14, red)*. Secure the thread to set the tension but don't trim.

**BACKING** Back the strip with Ultrasuede as in Step 3. note: *Lay the strip down on the Ultrasuede so that it curves to the right when the I bead at the tip points down.* Set the long base aside.

**5 rope.** Use odd-count tubular peyote stitch to create the rope:

**ROUND 1** Use 6' (1.8 m) of waxed thread to string 9A; pass through the first 3 beads strung, leaving a 5" (12.7 cm) tail *(fig. 15, blue)*.

**ROUND 2** String 1A, skip 1A previously strung, and pass through the next A; repeat three times to add a total of 4A *(fig. 15, red)*. **note:** *No step up is required; the rope will gradually spiral.*

**ROUNDS 3 AND ON** Work 1A in each stitch until the rope measures 13¼" (33.7 cm) or the desired length *(fig. 16)*. Use tight, consistent tension. You will need to add new lengths of thread to achieve the finished size; be sure to wax each new thread added.

**END** Work 1 more round with 1A in each stitch to add 5 more A *(fig. 15, blue)*. Without adding a bead, pass through the next A to form a decrease. Work 1 stitch with 1A. Without adding a bead, pass through the next A to form another decrease. Work 1 stitch with 1A. Work 2 stitches with 1A in each stitch *(fig. 17, red)*. Pass through the beads at the end of the rope to secure the end. Don't trim the thread.

**CLASP CONNECTION** Stitch the last ¼" (.6 cm) of the rope to the back of 1 purple/copper leaf, positioning it at the top of the leaf and passing through B and E beads *(fig. 18, blue)*. Stitch the eye half of the clasp to B and E beads on the back of the leaf, just below the end of the rope *(fig. 18, red)*. Secure the thread and trim. **note:** *The leaf will extend about ¾" (1.9 cm) beyond the end of the rope so the clasp will be concealed when worn.*

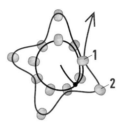

fig. 15: starting the rope with rounds 1 and 2

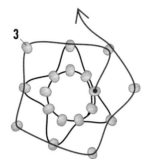

fig. 16: continuing in odd-count tubular peyote

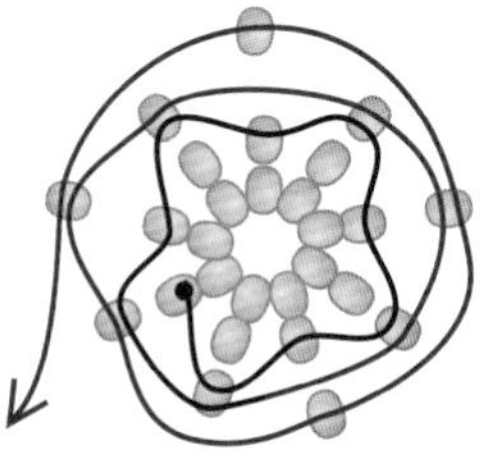

fig. 17: decreasing the final rounds of the rope

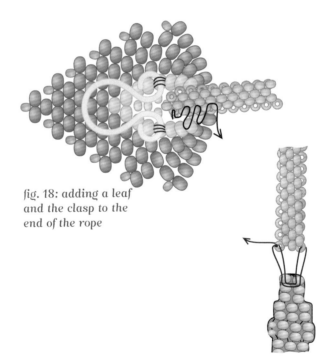

fig. 18: adding a leaf and the clasp to the end of the rope

fig. 19: attaching the starting end of the rope to the short base

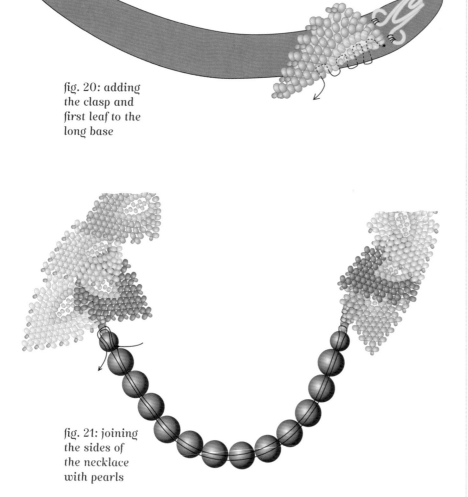

fig. 20: adding
the clasp and
first leaf to the
long base

fig. 21: joining
the sides of
the necklace
with pearls

**SHORT-BASE CONNECTION** Add a
needle to the rope's tail thread,
pass down through 1D at the top
end of the short base, and up
through the next. Pass through
1A on the opposite side of the
rope, back through the 2D,
and through the first A exited
*(fig. 19)*. Set this portion of the
necklace aside.

## TIPS

● Make a photocopy of the leaf
pattern and mark off beads as you
add them to keep track of your
progress.

● Try to use consistent tension
while stitching the rope so
it remains equally flexible
throughout.

● Use a snap set or a lobster or
spring-ring clasp with a closed
(soldered) jump ring, in place of
the hook-and-loop closure.

● The small hook-and-loop set
used here is more commonly used
for clothing. Find these sets in the
notions department of your sewing
store.

● See page 69 for more
information on making and
finishing tubular-peyote ropes.

**6** **assembly**. Add leaves to the bases and connect the center of the necklace with pearls:

**CLASP** Sew the hook half of the clasp to the Ultrasuede side of the long base, positioning the clasp at the top and stitching down through the Ultrasuede. Occasionally pass through adjacent base beads for added stability *(fig. 20, blue)*. Secure the thread and trim. The Ultrasuede will remain faceup when attaching the following leaves.

**LONG BASE** Add a needle to the thread of 1 dark steel/silver sage leaf and stitch it to the top of the long base, positioning it so it slightly conceals the hook half of the clasp. Close the clasp to check that the leaf added to the end of the rope in Step 5 will nicely overlap the dark steel/silver sage leaf. Pass through beads of the leaf, the Ultrasuede, and an occasional base bead to secure the leaf *(fig. 20, red)*. Add 1 more dark steel/silver sage leaf, 2 purple/copper leaves, 1 gray mist leaf, and 1 matte sage leaf to the base in the same manner, positioning them as desired or following the photograph.

**SHORT BASE** Add the 5 remaining leaves to the short base as before, stitching the top leaf to the end rounds of the rope to conceal the rope-to-base connection.

**PEARLS** Use 2' (.6 m) of waxed thread to string one 6mm pearl and pass through the I of the short base, leaving a 4" (10.2 cm) tail. Pass back through the 6mm pearl. String twelve 8mm pearls and the remaining 6mm pearl; pass through the I of the long base and back through the 13 beads just added. Tie a square knot with the tail thread, pass through the first 6mm pearl strung, and the I of the short base *(fig. 21)*. Repeat the thread path several times. Secure the threads and trim.

## DESIGN OPTION

● Diagonal peyote stitch is the perfect technique to use when creating a coordinating bracelet band for this project. The pointed ends formed by this peyote variation perfectly mirror the shape of the leaves. Here, 3 purple/copper leaves were stitched to the chartreuse band in different directions for a natural look, with two connected to one end of the band and one to the other end. A snap makes a great concealed closure for the overlapping elements, with one half stitched behind a leaf and the other to the band.

# circular peyote

Simply said, circular peyote stitch consists of a series of increases (or decreases) that keep the beadwork flat as it expands (or contracts) round by round into a disc or ring. And, of course, there are variations within this variation—try making ruffles, stacking circles to make buttons, and more.

My **Making Waves** necklace proves you only need to know one stitch to create rich and luscious jewelry. A handful of circular peyote discs, each edged with Thai silver rondelles to create subtle ruffles, are cleverly layered to give the necklace irresistible texture.

Make two star-motif discs using circular peyote stitch, stack them, and join them into petite buttonlike coins in my **Big Sky Bracelets**. Decrease stitches worked along the outside edges create openings that allow the reversible coins to be strung on strips of leather.

Melanie Potter's **Patterned Petals** necklace demonstrates how you can create patterns in your beadwork with careful planning and a little colorplay. The front and back of each disc is topped off with a bezeled crystal, making the components totally reversible.

*Enjoy the meditative repetition of this stitch as you work around and around and around.*

## TECHNIQUES

### counting

If working from the inside of a ring to the outside, the innermost round is Round 1 *(fig. 01)*.

If working from outside to inside, the outermost up beads make up Round 1 *(fig. 02)*. Always count the rounds in a zigzag pattern (not just along one line of beads).

### circular peyote stitch

Most circular peyote pieces are worked from the inside out because it is often easier to control the shape of the beadwork by working increases instead of decreases.

When stitching a disc with a very small opening in the center, make the first set of beads strung all Round 1 beads. For example, string 5 beads and tie a square knot to form a circle. Pass through the first bead strung, making sure the knot doesn't slip inside the bead. These are your Round 1 beads *(fig. 03, blue)*.

Now, to work Round 2, string 1 bead and pass through the next bead of Round 1. note: *You are not skipping over any beads of Round 1; you are adding 1 bead between each bead of Round 1.* Step up at the end of this round and all following rounds unless otherwise noted by passing through the first bead added *(fig. 03, red)*.

Notice how Round 2 is worked with the same technique regardless if you start with an odd or even number of beads in Round 1. Here Round 1 contains 6 beads. *(fig. 04)*.

For a ring (or any shape that requires a larger opening), the first

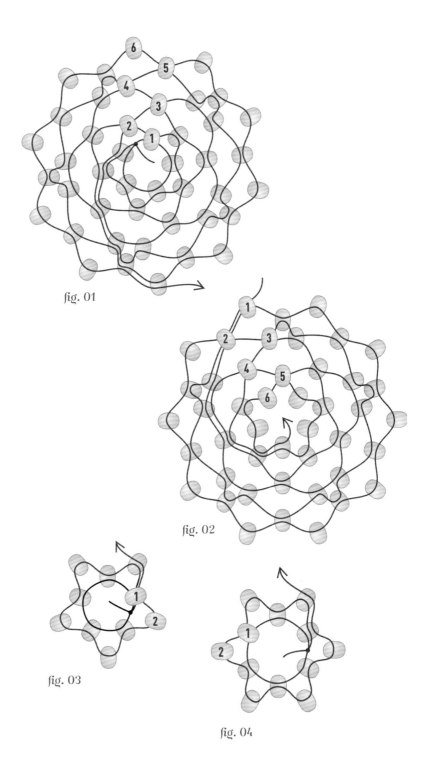

fig. 01

fig. 02

fig. 03

fig. 04

47

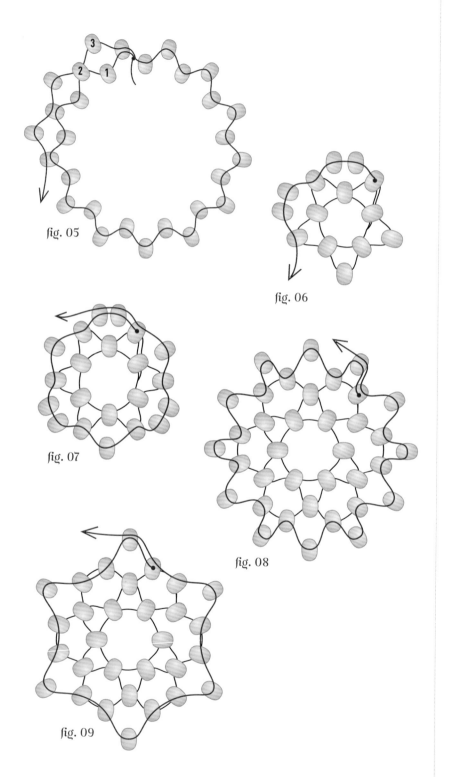

fig. 05

fig. 06

fig. 07

fig. 08

fig. 09

set of beads strung makes up both Rounds 1 and 2. Always start with an even number of beads. When adding the Round 3 beads, follow the peyote mantra: "String 1 bead, skip 1 bead, and pass through the next" *(fig. 05)*. Step up for each new round.

## increases

Working increases is an integral part of circular peyote stitch. Their main function is to grow the size of the beadwork. A large number of increases cause the work to ruffle, few increases cause the work to cup, and a moderate number of increases keep the work flat.

To work an increase round, work 2 beads in each stitch *(fig. 06)*.

Alternate increase rounds with 1 or 2 rounds that have just 1 bead in each stitch to grow the size of the circle. Since all beads vary slightly in size, you may have to play around with the number (or even types) of beads added in the increase rounds.

For a more gradual increase, alternate stitches worked with 1 bead with stitches worked with 2 beads. If your initial ring consists of both Round 1 and 2 beads (as in *fig. 05*), this works best with a total number of starting beads that is divisible by four *(fig. 07)*.

Depending on how you desire the beadwork to take shape, you may want to stitch the next round by adding 1 bead between each bead of the previous round (splitting the pairs of increase beads) *(fig. 08)*. Or, you may want to treat the 2 increase beads as 1 *(fig. 09)*.

*note: See Melanie Potter's Patterned Petals necklace for a great example of how to work just the right number of increases into a perfectly flat circular peyote-stitch disc. And see how increases are designed to encourage gentle cupping of the beadwork in the beaded coins in my Big Sky Bracelets.*

## decreases

To work a decrease, take a stitch without adding a bead, passing from 1 down bead of the previous round to the next. For a rapid decrease, work a decrease in every other stitch **(fig.10)**. Experiment with other combinations by decreasing in every other or every third stitch—it all depends on the shape you want to achieve.

See page 22 for the way to increase or decrease the size of the work by changing bead size instead of stitch count.

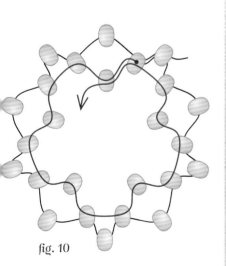

fig. 10

## STITCHING DURABLE BEADWORK
### How to Create and Care for Lasting Jewelry

Follow these simple stitching tips and care guidelines to keep the jewelry you devoted hours into making looking brand new. Don't forget to share this information with any non-beaders you gift or sell your work to; they might not be as familiar with the amazing yet often delicate architecture behind beadwoven jewelry.

● Store pieces flat or rested on neck forms. Hanging a beaded rope or strap on a small jewelry hook can stretch the thread that joins the beads beyond repair.

● Never stitch with a damaged thread. If you see a thread fray, replace it immediately to avoid weak spots. Wax can help prevent fraying, but, if your thread is synthetic, be sure to inquire about its archival quality with its manufacturer.

● Keep the work flexible. Beads can break easily when pieces made with too tight tension are manipulated. After every 2 or 3 rows or rounds worked, very gently twist and turn the beadwork to keep it a bit malleable.

● Always prestretch nylon threads. Otherwise, the thread will stretch after you finish, resulting in loose beads.

● End your thread after completing intricate components and before starting clasps. If a thread does break between components or at a connection point, you'll be left with an easy repair.

● Double your thread when stitching crystals and other sharp-holed beads. This way, if one thread breaks, you'll have a little more time to repair the damage before the second breaks and you lose your bead.

● Reinforce, reinforce, and reinforce areas joined by magnets so they can withstand repetitive pulling.

● There are two theories when it comes to thread length: 1) Use long thread to reduce the number of knots in the work; knots can create weak points. 2) Use short length of threads to cut down on tangling and the wear and tear caused by passing through beads multiple times. Personally, I'm in the second camp, but please find what works for you.

● Never trim a thread next to a knot; it will always find a way to come undone. Instead, weave back through several beads after tying the knot and before ending the thread.

● Be sure your thread size is appropriate for the job at hand. Thin threads may break too easily. Thick thread may make your work rigid or fill your beads too quickly, which prevents you from making multiple passes.

Create a richly textured collar by beading a handful of easy-to-stitch circular peyote–stitch coins, stacking them, and joining the ends. Depending on which colors and bead finishes you choose, this design can work for special occasions or casual events. Repeating circles mimic the waves of little stones skipping across water. ● *by melinda barta*

# making waves

## TECHNIQUES
Circular peyote stitch

Picot

Square stitch

## MATERIALS
2 g bronze metallic size 15° Japanese seed beads (A)

2 g cabernet metallic iris size 15° Japanese seed beads (B)

6 g 24k gold electroplate size 11° Japanese seed beads (C)

4 g 24k gold matte metallic size 11° Japanese seed beads (D)

4 g gold bronze metallic iris size 11° Japanese seed beads (E)

2 g silver-lined dark gold size 11° Japanese seed beads (F)

3 g red copper metallic size 11° Japanese seed beads (G)

3 g rusty bronze matte metallic iris size 11° Japanese seed beads (H)

3 g raspberry metallic luster size 11° Japanese seed beads (I)

530 Thai silver 1.5×1mm flower-print rondelles (J)

1 Thai silver 3×2.5mm rondelle

Smoke 6 lb braided beading thread

## TOOLS
Scissors

Size 10 and 12 beading needles

51

**1 gold coins.** Use circular peyote stitch to create gold beaded coins. **note:** *Start with the size 10 needle and switch to the size 12 if you ever have trouble fitting the needle through beads.*

**ROUND 1** Use 18" (45.7 cm) of thread to string 5C, leaving a 2" (5.1 cm) tail. Tie a square knot with the tail and working threads to form a circle. Pass through all 5 beads again and exit the first bead added, making sure the knot doesn't slip inside the bead *(fig. 01, blue)*.

**ROUND 2** String 1F and pass through the next C of Round 1; repeat four times to add a total of 5F. Step up through the first F added in this round *(fig. 01, red)*.

**ROUND 3** Work 5 stitches with 2E in each stitch to add a total of 10E. Step up through the first E added in this round *(fig. 02, blue)*.

**ROUND 4** Work 1D in each stitch, splitting the pairs of E from Round 3 to form increases and adding a total of 10D. Step up through the first D added in this round *(fig. 02, red)*.

**ROUND 5** Work 1C in each stitch to add a total of 10C. Step up through the first C added in this round *(fig. 03, blue)*.

**ROUND 6** String 1A, 1J, and 1A, then pass through the next C of Round 5 to form a picot; repeat nine times to add a total of 20A and 10J *(fig. 03, blue)*. Repeat the entire thread path in this round to reinforce. Secure the tail

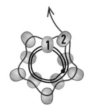

fig. 01: working rounds 1 and 2

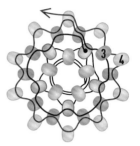

fig. 02: stitching rounds 3 and 4

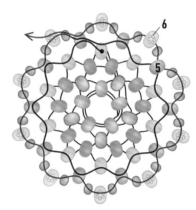

fig. 03: working rounds 5 and 6

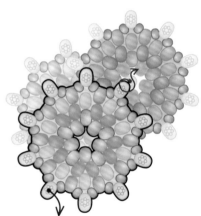

fig. 04: joining the first 2 gold coins

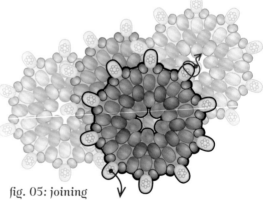

fig. 05: joining the first 2 cabernet coins

thread and trim; don't trim the working thread.

Repeat this entire step twenty-five times for a total of 26 gold coins. Set the coins aside.

## 2 cabernet coins. Repeat Step 1 using the following colors:

Use E for Round 1, G for Round 2, I for Round 3, H for Round 4, and G for Round 5. In Round 6, use 1B, 1J, and 1B in each stitch.

Repeat this entire step twenty-six times for a total of 27 cabernet coins. Set the coins aside.

## 3 connections. Join the coins by square-stitching rondelles together through the opening in Round 1:

**FIRST GOLD CONNECTION** Add a needle to the working thread on 1 gold coin; pass through the hole in the center of Round 1 of 1 cabernet coin. Pass through 1J of Round 6 on a second gold coin, making sure this J is opposite the J with the thread *(fig. 04, blue)* coming out of it. Position the coins in your hand as they are stacked in *fig. 4*. Square-stitch together the Js of the 2 gold coins, continuing to pass through just the opening in the cabernet coin and not through any of that coin's beads *(fig. 04, red)*. Repeat the thread path several times. Secure the thread and trim. Fold up the last coin added to begin forming a single row of coins.

**FIRST CABERNET CONNECTION**
*Add a needle to the thread of the last cabernet coin added. Pass through the hole in the center of the last gold coin added. Pass through 1J of Round 6 on a new cabernet coin, making sure this J is opposite the J with the thread *(fig. 05, blue)* coming out of it. Position the coins in your hand as they are stacked in *fig. 05*. Square-stitch together the Js of the 2 cabernet coins as before *(fig. 05, red)*. Repeat the thread path several times. Secure the thread and trim. Fold up the last coin added.

**SECOND GOLD CONNECTION** Add a needle to the thread of the last gold coin added. Join a new gold coin as before, stitching through the center of the last cabernet coin added.

**SECOND CABERNET CONNECTION** Repeat instructions for the first cabernet connection, but this time rotate the new cabernet coin counterclockwise by 1J so that the J with the thread *(fig. 06, blue)* coming out of it has 5 free J to the left of it and 3 free J to the right of it *(fig. 06)*. **note:** *This establishes the curve of the collar.*

**THIRD GOLD CONNECTION** Repeat as for the second gold connection. Set 1 cabernet coin aside to use for the clasp. Repeat from * until all the coins are joined, continuing to rotate every other cabernet coin in the same direction for the curved neckline. Secure and trim the thread on the last cabernet coin added.

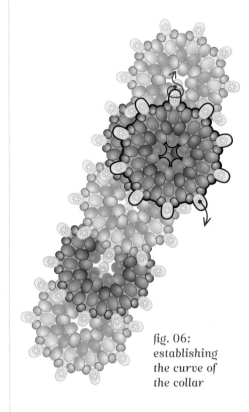

*fig. 06: establishing the curve of the collar*

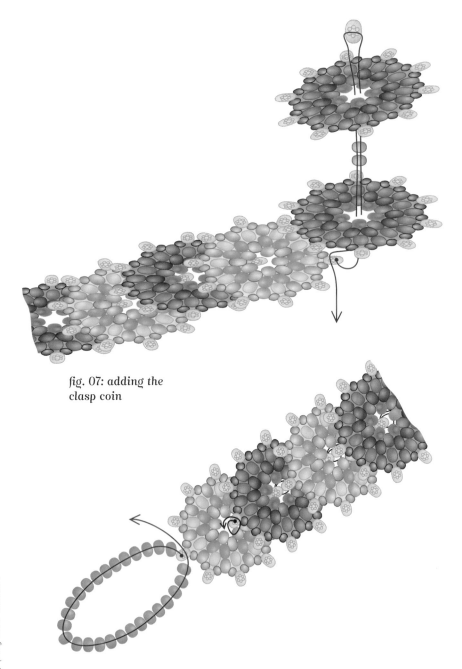

fig. 07: adding the
clasp coin

fig. 08: connecting the first 2 coins
and adding the clasp loop

**4** **clasp.** Create the closure out of 2 stacked cabernet coins and a loop of seed beads:

**COIN** Use the thread of the final gold coin to pass through the center of the collar's final cabernet coin. String 2F; pass through the center of the remaining cabernet coin. String the 3×2.5mm rondelle; pass back through the center of the last cabernet coin added, the 2F, and the center of the collar's final cabernet coin. Pass through the last J exited *(fig. 07)*. Repeat the thread path twice to reinforce. Secure the thread and trim. note: *The clasp loop will rest between the 2 stacked cabernet coins.*

**LOOP** Start 12" (30.5 cm) of new thread that exits the J of the first cabernet coin opposite the J that connects to the second cabernet coin. Square-stitch that J to the nearest bead of Round 1 in the first gold coin *(fig. 08, blue)*. Weave through beads to exit the J of the first gold coin at the end of the collar. String 27E (or enough to slip over the last cabernet coin added without being too loose); pass through the last J exited *(fig. 08, red)*. Repeat the thread path twice to reinforce. Secure the thread and trim.

## TIPS

● If you have good eyesight and a steady hand, this tip will save you a little time: After you finish Round 1, pass the tail end of the thread (without adding a needle) through 1 or 2 beads. Since the braided beading thread is somewhat stiff, you can usually do this without the needle. Trim the thread close to

the beadwork, and you won't have a tail thread to deal with later.

● If you're hesitant to venture out into the world of color alone, look for seed bead mixes from your favorite bead supplier. Let someone else's "bead soup" give you a jump start on a color blend and then add other shades you love to make it your own.

## DESIGN OPTIONS

● For coins with a little more ruffle, use larger beads in place of the 1.5×1mm rondelles. In this sage green–and-navy bracelet, I used 2mm Thai silver cornerless cubes in place of J in Round 6. I joined the coins according to the collar instructions to give the bracelet a gentle curve. Because of this, the bracelet drapes nicely over the base of the wrist. The modern cornerless cubes and increased number of matte-finished beads give this design a more casual look.

● Instead of making your own clasp in Step 4, use a premade one. In this purple-and-aqua bracelet variation, I attached a flower-and-leaf 14x28mm pewter hook-and-loop clasp. I didn't offset the coins (as in the collar) so the design follows a straight line.

Reversible circular peyote-stitch coins, strung on leather for a little western flair, slide up and down these fun double-wrapped bracelets. Or, instead of wrapping the adorned leather strands around your wrist, wear this design as a choker. The style is fit for an adventurous vacation at a Big Sky, Montana, ranch or a casual weekend in the city. ● *by melinda barta*

# big sky bracelets

## TECHNIQUES
Circular and tubular peyote stitch

Wirework (Sunrise colorway only)

Zipping

## MATERIALS
*Sunrise Colorway*
2 g each size 11° Japanese seed beads in russet rose permanent galvanized, copper coral Durocoat galvanized, and mauve permanent galvanized (A)

7 g leaf matte metallic size 11° Japanese seed beads (B)

1 brass 1½" (3.8 cm) ball-end head pin with 2.5mm ball

3' (.9 m) of natural light brown 2mm round leather cord

Smoke 6 lb braided beading thread

*Twilight Colorway*
1 g each size 11° Japanese seed beads in silver sage matte permanent galvanized, dark steel/silver sage permanent galvanized, gray mist matte metallic, and 24k gold matte metallic (A)

7 g purple/copper matte metallic iris size 11° Japanese seed beads (B)

Optional: 1 g 24k gold size 11° Japanese seed beads (C)

3' (.9 m) of chocolate 5×1mm deertan flat lace cord

Smoke 6 lb braided beading thread

## TOOLS
Scissors

Size 10 beading needle

Chain- or flat-nose pliers

Round-nose pliers and wire cutters (Sunrise colorway only)

## FINISHED SIZE
Adjustable

## NOTE
*The instructions for the Sunrise and Twilight colorways only differ when choosing a finishing technique in Steps 4 and 5. Figures 1–8 feature a coin in the Sunrise colorway.*

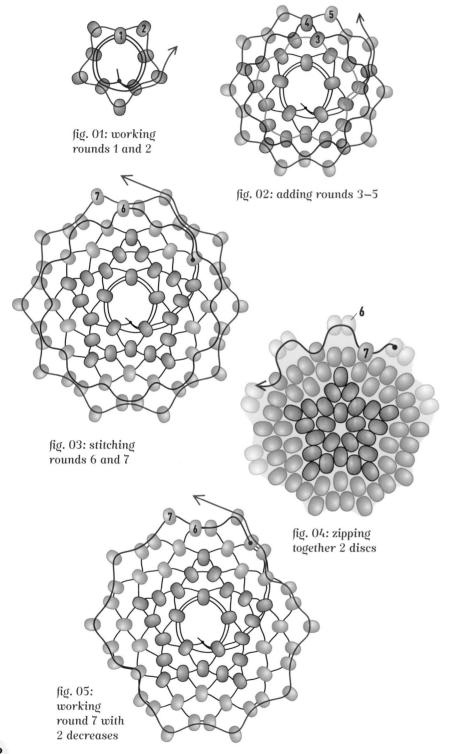

fig. 01: working
rounds 1 and 2

fig. 02: adding rounds 3–5

fig. 03: stitching
rounds 6 and 7

fig. 04: zipping
together 2 discs

fig. 05:
working
round 7 with
2 decreases

**1 clasp coin.** Use circular peyote stitch to make 2 circles and join them along the outside edge to form the coin that will serve as the clasp. **note:** *Choose one of the colors labeled A and use this color for all the A beads on this first side of the coin.*

**ROUND 1** Use 20" (50.8 cm) of thread to string 5A. Tie a square knot with the tail and working threads to form a circle. Pass through all 5 beads again and exit the first bead added, making sure the knot doesn't slip inside the bead *(fig. 01, blue)*.

**ROUND 2** String 1A and pass through the next A of Round 1; repeat four times to add a total of 5A. Step up through the first bead added in this round *(fig. 01, red)*.

**ROUND 3** Work 5 stitches with 2A in each stitch to add a total of 10A. Step up through the first bead added in this round *(fig. 02, green)*.

**ROUND 4** String 1A, pass through the next A of Round 3 (splitting the pair of beads), string 1B, and pass through the next A of Round 3; repeat this entire sequence four times to add a total of 5A and 5B. Step up through the first bead added in this round *(fig. 02, blue)*.

**ROUND 5** Work 1B in each stitch to add a total of 10B. Step up through the first bead added in this round *(fig. 02, red)*.

**ROUND 6** Work 10 stitches with 2B in each stitch to add a total of 20B. Step up through the first 2 beads added in this round *(fig. 03, blue)*.

**ROUND 7** Work 1B in each stitch, treating the 2B of Round 6 as one bead, to add a total of 10B. Step up through the first bead added in this round *(fig. 03, red)*. Don't trim the thread. Set the clasp coin aside.

Using a different color of A of your choice, repeat Rounds 1–6 for a second circle.

**ZIP** Exit 2B of Round 6 on the second circle. Pass through 1B of Round 7 on the first circle and the next 2B of Round 6 on the second circle *(fig. 04)*; repeat around to zip the 2 sides together. Use tight tension so the single B beads added in Round 7 on the first circle are on the outside edge of the coin. Repeat the thread path at least once; secure the thread and trim. Use the thread of the first circle to repeat the thread path along the outside edge again for reinforcement; secure the thread and trim. Set the clasp coin aside.

**2 slider coins.** Create coins as for the clasp coin, but form an opening to accommodate the cord.

**ROUNDS 1–6** Repeat Step 1, Rounds 1–6 using the color of A of your choice. **note:** *For the Twilight colorway, use a few C in place of the gold A beads for a bit of sparkle, if desired.*

**ROUND 7** Work 4 stitches with 1B in each stitch, treating the 2B of Round 6 as 1 bead. Without adding a bead, pass through the nearest bead of Round 5 and the next 2B of Round 6 to form a decrease *(fig. 05, blue)*. Repeat the entire sequence to add a grand total of 8 beads in this round. Step up through the first bead added in this round *(fig. 05, red)*. Don't trim the thread. Set aside.

Using a different color of A of your choice, repeat Rounds 1–6 for a second circle.

**ZIP** Exit 2B in Round 6 on the second circle. Pass through 1B of Round 7 on the first circle and the next 2B of Round 6 on the second circle; repeat around to zip the 2 sides together. **note:** *When you reach the decrease in the first circle's Round 7, weave through beads to reach the next 2B pair and continue zipping the sides (fig. 06); this forms the first opening in the coin that will later accommodate the cords.* Use tight tension as before. Repeat the thread path twice; secure the thread and trim. Use the thread of the first circle to repeat the thread path along the outside edge again for reinforcement; secure the thread and trim. **note:** *Be sure to pass through the Round 7 beads from both sides of the coin to reinforce the opening (fig. 07, blue and red).* Set the slider coin aside.

Repeat this entire step six times for a total of 7 slider coins using different colors for the A beads as desired.

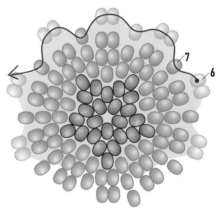

fig. 06: zipping together 2 discs with decreases

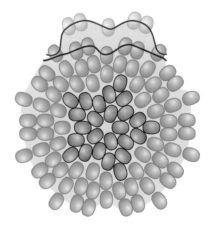

fig. 07: bird's-eye view of opening

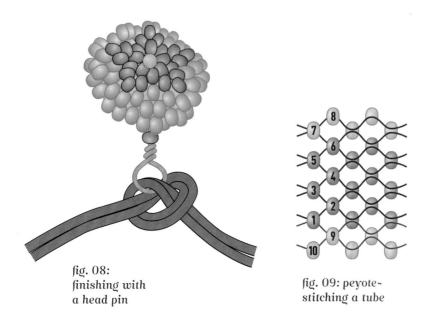

fig. 08:
finishing with
a head pin

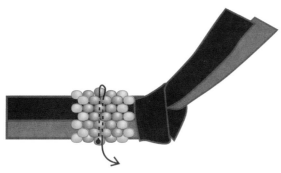

fig. 09: peyote-
stitching a tube

fig. 10: stitching a
tube in place

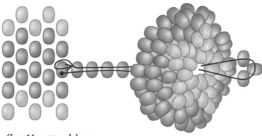

fig. 11: attaching
the clasp coin

back of head
pin finish

**3 cord.** Use leather cord to
string the coins:

**CLASP LOOP** Fold the cord in half
and use an overhand knot to form
a ¾" (1.9 cm) loop at the end.
Check to make sure the clasp coin
will easily pass through the loop
and that the loop isn't too large.

**STRINGING** Use both cord ends
(stack the ends if using the flat
lace cord) to string 1 coin. If
needed, gently increase the size
of a coin opening by inserting the
tip of a closed pair of chain- or
flat-nose pliers in the opening
and then releasing the pliers.
Repeat to string the remaining
coins, arranging the colors in a
pleasing manner.

**END KNOT** Join the cord ends and
use both to tie an overhand knot.
Choose one of the two following
finishing techniques.

**4 head pin finish.** Attach
the clasp coin using simple
wirework as shown in the Sunrise
colorway or skip to Step 5 for an
alternate finish:

Slightly loosen the end knot. Use the head pin to string the clasp coin, passing through the opening in the center of Round 1, and string 1A. Form a wrapped loop that attaches to 2 cords near the center of the knot *(fig. 08)*. Pull the knot to retighten.

# 5 peyote tubes finish.

Attach the clasp coin using tubular peyote stitch as shown in the Twilight colorway:

**ROUNDS 1 AND 2** Leaving a 9" (22.9 cm) tail, use 18" (45.7 cm) of thread to string 10B, wrap the strand around the cord near the end knot, and pass through 10 beads again. Tie a square knot with the tail and working threads to form a circle. Pass through the first bead, making sure the knot doesn't slip inside the bead.

**ROUND 3** String 1B, skip 1B previously strung, and pass through the next B; repeat four times to add a total of 5B. Step up for each new round by passing through the first bead added in the current round.

**ROUNDS 4–6** Work 1B in each stitch to add a total of 5B in each of 3 rounds.

**ROUNDS 7 AND 8** Work 1A in each stitch to add a total of 5A in each of 2 rounds *(fig. 09, blue)*. Secure the thread and trim.

**ROUNDS 9 AND 10** Use the tail thread to repeat Round 7, working off the beads of Round 1. Repeat Round 7 again *(fig. 09, red)*. Weave through beads to exit a B of Round 4.

**TACK** Pass through the leather to the other side of the tube, pass through a bead of Round 4, and back through the leather *(fig. 10)*. Repeat the thread path to reinforce and secure the tube in place. Use a needle puller or pair of chain- or flat-nose pliers as needed to help guide the needle through the leather.

**CLASP COIN** String 4B, pass through the opening created by Round 1 in the clasp coin, and string 3B; pass back through the center of the coin and the first 4B strung. Pass through the last bead exited on the tube *(fig. 11)*. Repeat the thread path at least twice to reinforce. Secure the thread and trim.

Repeat Rounds 1–10 and Tack instructions just before the knot that forms the clasp loop.

## TIPS

● If it feels like your leather knots will loosen, secure them with inconspicuous dabs of jeweler's adhesive.

● These bracelets are designed to wrap around your wrist twice, but sliding all the coins next to each other in a single-wrap bracelet is a great option, too.

Peyote tube finish on the Twilight colorway

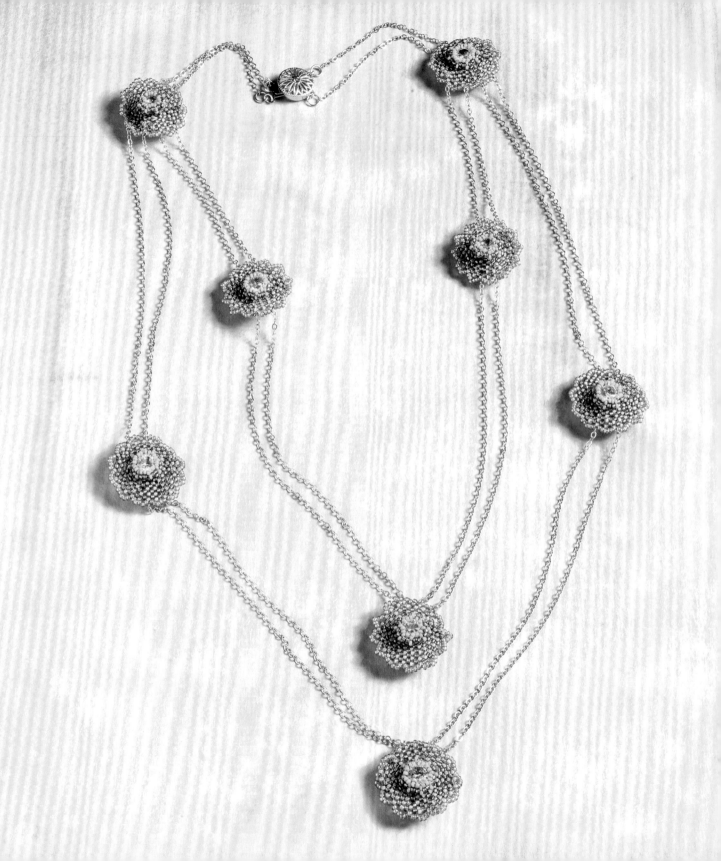

The clever placement of different-colored beads creates the subtle checkered pattern in this flowing neckpiece's flower discs. The discs are reversible in case one happens to flip, and, best of all, the light drape of the chain feels so good around your neck. Use circular peyote stitch to form the petals and tubular peyote stitch for the bezels. ● *by melanie potter*

# patterned petals

**TECHNIQUES**
Circular and tubular peyote stitch

**MATERIALS**
8 g metallic teal–lined clear size 15° Japanese seed beads (A)

8 g sage green–lined amber size 15° Japanese seed beads (B)

5 g lavender-lined clear AB size 15° Japanese seed beads (C)

5 g chartreuse size 15° Czech charlottes (D)

2 g sage green–lined amber size 11° Japanese seed beads (E)

16 jonquil or canary yellow SS29 (about 6mm) pointed-back faceted round crystal chatons or cubic zirconias

79" (2 m) of gold-filled 1.5×2mm flat cable chain

1 gold-filled 12mm 2-strand round filigree box clasp with 3mm soldered jump rings

4 gold-filled 4mm jump rings

Pale blue size B nylon beading thread

Beading wax

**TOOLS**
Scissors

Size 12 beading needle

2 pairs of chain- or flat-nose pliers

Bead mat

**FINISHED SIZE**
22" (55.9 cm) (shortest strand); 28" (71.1 cm) (longest strand)

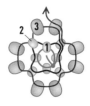

*fig. 01: stitching
rounds 1–3*

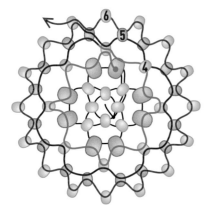

*fig. 02: adding
rounds 4–6*

**1 disc.** Use circular peyote stitch to make a patterned disc:

**DISC ROUND 1** Use 65" (1.7 m) of waxed thread to string 4A, leaving a 26" (66 cm) tail. Tie a square knot with the tail and working threads to form a circle. Pass through the first A strung, making sure the knot doesn't slip inside the bead *(fig. 01, green)*.

**DISC ROUND 2** String 1A and pass through the next A of Round 1; repeat three times to add a total of 4A. Unless otherwise noted, step up for each new round by passing through the first bead added in the current round *(fig. 01, blue)*.

**DISC ROUND 3** Work 4 stitches with 2E in each stitch to add a total of 8E *(fig. 01, red)*. note: *Continue to step up through just the first bead added in the following rounds even if you added 2 beads in each stitch.*

**DISC ROUND 4** Work 1A in each stitch to add a total of 8A, splitting the pairs of 2E from Round 3 *(fig. 02, green)*.

**DISC ROUND 5** Work 8 stitches with 2B in each stitch to add a total of 16B *(fig. 02, blue)*.

**DISC ROUND 6** Work 1A in each stitch, splitting the pairs of 2B from Round 5 and stitching a bead between each pair, to add a total of 16A *(fig. 02, red)*.

**DISC ROUND 7** Work 1B in each stitch to add a total of 16B *(fig. 03, green)*.

**DISC ROUND 8** Work 1 stitch with 1A and 1 stitch with 2A; repeat this entire sequence seven times to add a total of 24A *(fig. 03, blue)*.

**DISC ROUND 9** Work 1B in each stitch, splitting the pairs of 2A from Round 8 and working 2 stitches with 1B in between each pair, to add a total of 24B *(fig. 03, red)*.

**DISC ROUND 10** Work 1A in each stitch to add a total of 24A *(fig. 04, green)*.

**DISC ROUND 11** Work 1B in each stitch to add a total of 24B *(fig. 04, blue)*.

**DISC ROUND 12 (SCALLOPS)** String 5C, skip 1B of Round 11, and pass through the next B; repeat eleven times to add a total of 12 scallops *(fig. 04, red)*. Step up through the first 5C added. Don't trim the thread.

**2 bezel.** Use tubular peyote stitch to bezel a crystal stone that attaches to the disc:

**BEZEL ROUND 1** Add a needle to the tail thread and weave through beads to exit an E of Disc Round 3. Working off Disc Round 3, work 1A in each stitch to add a total of 8A *(fig. 05, purple)*. Unless otherwise noted, step up for each new round by

---

**TIP**

● Don't pull the tension tight when working the first 3 rounds in Step 1 or it will be difficult to pass through the E beads of Disc Round 3 when stitching the second bezel.

passing through the first bead added in the current round.

**BEZEL ROUND 2** Work 1B in each stitch to add a total of 8B *(fig. 05, green)*.

**BEZEL ROUND 3** Work 8 stitches with 2A in each stitch to add a total of 16A. Step up through the first 2A added *(fig. 05, blue)*. note: *Test the fit of a crystal stone, and if you find that your bezel is not tight enough, remove the beads of this round and rework it, alternating between 1 stitch with 2A and 1 stitch with 1A.*

**BEZEL ROUND 4** Work 1D in each stitch, treating the 2A of Bezel Round 3 as 1 bead to add a total of 8D *(fig. 05, red)*.

**INSERT STONE** Insert 1 crystal stone so the previous rounds rest against the back of the stone.

**BEZEL ROUND 5** As you work this inside round of the bezel, hold the stone in place with the thumb of your nondominant hand. Use firm tension to tighten up the work as you stitch, pulling the beadwork toward the center of the bezel. Work 1 stitch with 2D and 1 stitch with 1D; repeat three times to add a total of 12D. Don't step up; exit 2A of Bezel Round 3 *(fig. 06, blue)*.

**BEZEL ROUND 6** Work 1D in each stitch, treating the 2A of Bezel Round 3 as 1 bead to add a total of 8D *(fig. 06, red)*.

Weave through beads to exit the other side of the disc from Disc Round 3. Repeat the bezel instructions on the other side of the disc.

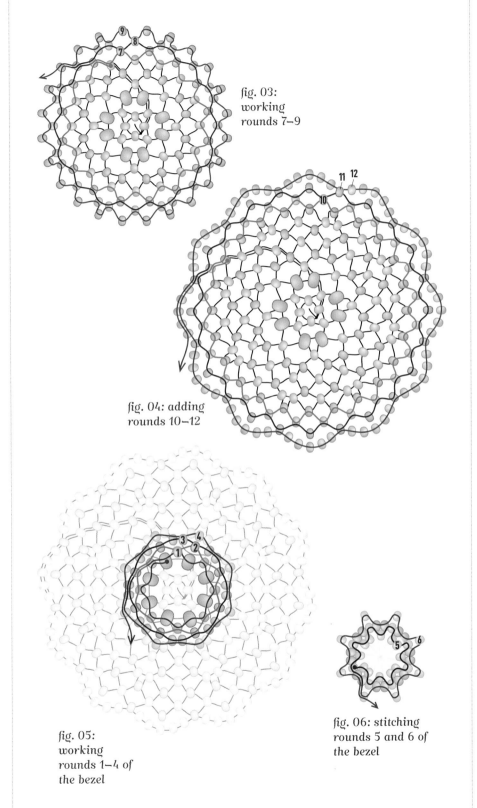

fig. 03: working rounds 7–9

fig. 04: adding rounds 10–12

fig. 05: working rounds 1–4 of the bezel

fig. 06: stitching rounds 5 and 6 of the bezel

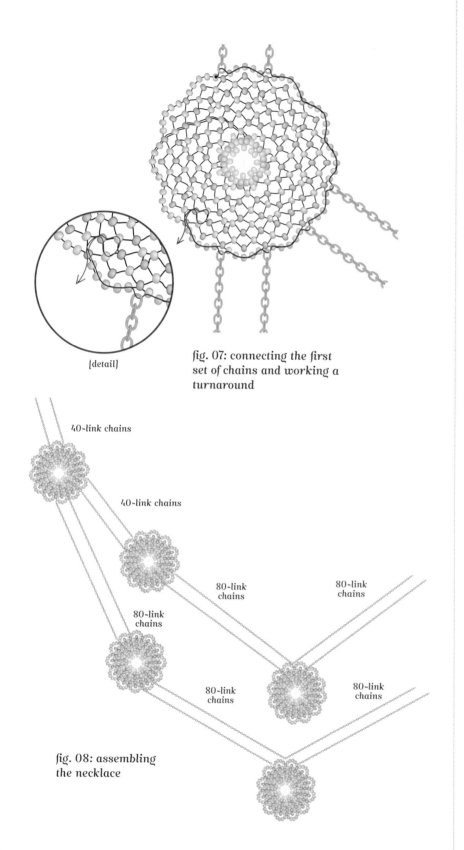

fig. 07: connecting the first
set of chains and working a
turnaround

[detail]

40-link chains

40-link chains

80-link
chains

80-link
chains

80-link
chains

80-link
chains

80-link
chains

80-link
chains

fig. 08: assembling
the necklace

note: *Bezel Round 1 on the second side
will be a little tight so use the flat-nose
pliers to help push and pull the needle
through beads.* Secure the tail thread
and trim; don't cut the working
thread attached to Disc Round 12.

Repeat Steps 1 and 2 seven times
for a total of 8 discs.

**3 assembly.** Join the discs
with segments of chain:
**CUTTING** Lay the chain out on the
bead mat and hold down one end
by putting a needle into the first
link. Count out 40 links and cut
the forty-first link. Repeat seven
times for a total of eight 40-link
segments. **note:** *If using different-
sized chain, cut these segments to*

mastering peyote stitch

2⅜" (6 cm). Cut twelve 80-link segments in the same manner. **note:** *If using different-sized chain, cut these segments to 4⅞" (12.4 cm).*

**CONNECT DISCS** Using the original working thread, string the free end of one 40-link chain and pass through the next 5C of Disc Round 12. String the free end of a second 40-link chain. Weave through beads of Disc Rounds 11 and 12 to exit 3 scallops away. String the free end of one 40-link chain and pass through the next 5C of Disc Round 12; repeat three times *(fig. 07, blue)*.

Work a turnaround to exit back through the last Disc Round 11 bead exited *(fig. 07, red)*. Weave back through all of the beads and chains to reinforce the connections. Secure the thread and trim. Connect all the remaining discs in the same manner, referring to *fig. 08* for chain lengths and placement on the left side of the necklace and center discs. Connect the right side of the necklace to mirror the left.

**CLASP CONNECTION** Use 1 jump ring to attach the final link of each end chain to a clasp ring, making sure the chains aren't twisted.

### DESIGN OPTION

● Create this sparkly silver colorway by pairing tanzanite chatons with amber-lined clear size 15°s and 11°s, purple AB size 15°s, silver-lined pearl size 15°s, and clear AB charlottes. Sterling silver chain, jump rings, and a clasp complete the look.

# tubular peyote

Tubular peyote stitch and circular peyote stitch are as alike as two peas in a pod because they are both worked in the round. But unlike circular peyote stitch (which most often remains flat), the beads of tubular peyote stitch stack on top of each other to form a dimensional object.

Bead-embroiderer extraordinaire Sherry Serafini shows us how to perfectly bezel cabochons using tubular peyote stitch. In her beautifully colored **Marcella Cuff,** she starts the first two rounds of each bezel on a beading foundation and then finishes off with more rounds of decorative seed beads.

Make all three of my **Geometry 101** bracelets or use the patterns presented here to make just one circle, triangle, or square component. Whether you use these beaded shapes as great pendants, clasps, or beaded beads, the know-how for making these shapes is invaluable. Thanks to just the right combination of size 15° and size 11° Japanese seed beads in my **Happy-Go-Lucky Links** necklace, it's possible to give basic beaded rings an oval shape. Stitch up a handful of ovals and link them together with flat-peyote rings to create a beaded chain interspersed with cheerful lampwork ovals.

*From bezels to ropes to rings, tubular peyote stitch is truly versatile.*

## TECHNIQUES

### counting

Always count the rounds in a diagonal or zigzag pattern (not just along one column of beads) as you would any other variation of peyote *(fig. 01)*.

Since the beads in odd-count tubes spiral slightly, it can be difficult to count rounds. Thus, it is easier to refer to long tubes by their overall length, not by the total number of rounds.

### illustrations

A note on tubular-peyote diagrams: The starting rounds of tubular peyote stitch are often illustrated like circular peyote stitch with a bird's-eye view (as seen in *fig. 02*); as the beadwork grows in size, the work is then shown with a side view (as seen in *fig. 01*).

### even-count tubular peyote stitch

String an even number of beads and tie a square knot to form a circle. This starting circle makes up Rounds 1 and 2. Pass through the first bead strung, making sure the knot doesn't slip inside the bead *(figs. 02 and 03, blue;* both bird's-eye and side views shown). For Round 3, follow the peyote mantra: "String 1 bead, skip 1 bead, and pass through the next." Step up at the end of this round, and all following rounds unless otherwise

noted, by passing through the first bead added (*figs. 02 and 03, red;* both bird's-eye and side views shown). Pull the beadwork so the Round 3 beads stack on top of the Round 1 beads.

Continue working each round with 1 bead in each stitch, remembering to step up at the end of each round *(fig. 04)*.

After working a few rounds, pull the thread tight to snug the beadwork and, if desired, slip the tube over a knitting needle, chopstick, wood skewer, dowel, etc., to hold the shape of the tube as you stitch. You may find this helpful when working the next 3 to 5 rounds and then you may feel you can go without it once the tube shape is set.

### odd-count tubular peyote stitch

Starting with an odd number of beads is great when creating a long beaded rope because no step ups are required.

#### basic rope

String an odd number of beads and tie a square knot to form a circle. This starting circle makes up Rounds 1 and 2. Pass through the first bead strung, making sure the knot doesn't slip inside the bead. For Round 3, follow the peyote mantra: "String 1 bead, skip 1 bead, and pass through the next." After you work your way around the starting circle *(fig. 05, blue)*, string 1 bead and pass through the first bead added in this round *(fig. 05, red)*. Pull the beadwork so the Round 3 beads stack on top of the Round 1 beads.

fig. 01

fig. 02

fig. 03

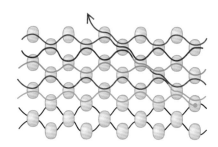

fig. 04

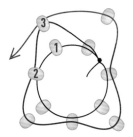

fig. 05

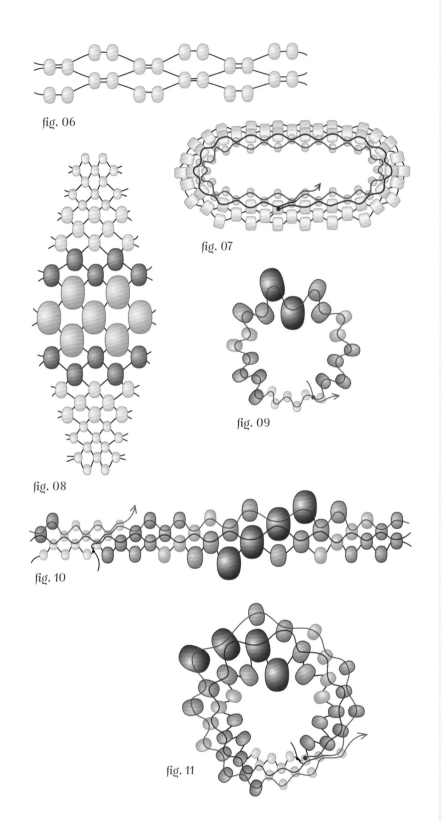

fig. 06

fig. 07

fig. 08

fig. 09

fig. 10

fig. 11

Continue working 1 bead in each stitch for the desired length.

## two-drop tubular peyote stitch

If working with 2 beads in each stitch, it's best to do so when forming large tubes. Otherwise, the pairs of beads can keep you from getting a nice, smooth edge on smaller tubes. If the work collapses, add a core of beads (see finishing tip on page 73) **(fig. 06)**.

## increases and decreases

Expand or contract the opening in the beaded tube by working the mid-row increase and decrease techniques starting on page 21. A large number of increases cause the work to ruffle; decreases cause the beadwork to cup and/or close up the end of a tube. Or, change bead size to shape the work.

### bead-size change for bezels

Tubular peyote is commonly used for bezeling crystal rivolis and cabochons. The outside wall of the bezel is created with a short tube of peyote, and then decreases are formed to hold the rivoli or cab in place. The easiest, cleanest, and most successful decreases in this application are created by downsizing beads. For example, if the body of the bezel is worked with size 11° seed beads or Delicas **(fig. 07, blue)**, simply work a few rounds with size 15°s **(fig. 07, red)**, and tight tension to pull the edges of the beadwork over the top (or bottom) of the rivoli or cab. Encourage the beadwork to cup while you stitch the rounds with the small beads by manipulating it with your fingers *(fig. 07)*.

### bead-size change in ropes

Create wide and narrow sections in a rope by graduating from small to large beads and then back to small. For the most dramatic texture, work several rounds of size 15° seed beads, then a few rounds of 11°s, 8°s, and 6°s, and then reverse the order. Maintain tight tension when working the 8°s and 6°s; using doubled 6 lb braided beading thread will help you achieve this. To help add flexibility to the work, use slightly looser tension in the section of 15°s. Make sure you choose a thread color that blends well with your beads as some thread may show between the size 8°s and 6°s *(fig. 08)*. note: *This works with both odd- and even-count ropes.*

### spirals

Just a few stitch and/or bead-size variations can add a playful twist to any tube of peyote stitch. Give these two a try.

### ribbed spiral

The thread path for this spiral is the same as even-count tubular peyote, but a mix of drastically different-sized beads causes the work to undulate and twist. If altering the pattern, just make sure you still have a good mix of bead sizes—the drastic difference in size between the smallest and largest beads is what creates the undulations. Learn the technique by following this sample, then play around with your own variations:

bead size changes in ropes

ribbed spiral

Dutch spiral

note: *Rounds 1–4 of this spiral are shown in both a bird's-eye and side view in **fig. 10** and **fig. 11**.*

**ROUNDS 1 AND 2** String 1 green size 15°, 2 indigo size 11°s, 2 red size 11°s, 2 teal size 11°s, 2 purple size 8°s, 2 blue size 6°s, 2 purple size 8°s, 2 teal size 11°s, 2 red size 11°s, 2 indigo size 11°s, 2 green size 15°s, 2 bronze size 15°s, and 1 green size 15°. Tie a square knot with the tail and working threads to form a circle. Pass through the first bead strung, making sure the knot doesn't slip inside the bead *(fig. 09)*.

**ROUND 3** String 1 green size 15°, skip 1 bead previously strung, and pass through the next bead. Repeat eleven times to add a total of 12 beads in this order: 1 indigo size 11°, 1 red size 11°, 1 teal size 11°, 1 purple size 8°, 1 blue size 6°, 1 purple size 8°, 1 teal size 11°, 1 red size 11°, 1 indigo size 11°, 1 green size 15°, and 1 bronze size 15°. note: *Step up for each new round by passing through the first bead added in the current round (figs. 10 and 11, blue)*.

**ROUND 4 AND ON** Work tubular peyote with 1 bead in each stitch to add a total of 12 beads in each round. To continue the spiral pattern, always string a bead identical to the one last exited *(figs. 10 and 11, red)*. Work with relaxed tension so the work doesn't become too stiff, but not so relaxed that any stitches are left loose.

### Dutch spiral

Familiarize yourself with this spin on tubular peyote and then play around with different bead counts and sizes to create a spiral with unexpected textures. The only difference between this stitch and odd-count tubular peyote is the addition of "float" beads. In this example, the 3 green size 15°s are strung before a size 11° in one stitch of each round, but they are never stitched into any of the following rounds. Thus, they float on the thread, adding decoration to the stitch and increasing flexibility in the tube. Depending on the size of your large accent beads (I used blue size 6°s here), you may want to increase or decrease the number of float beads. Learn the technique by following this sample. **note:** *Rounds 1–6 of this spiral are shown in both a bird's-eye and side view in* **fig. 13** *and* **fig. 14**.

**ROUNDS 1 AND 2** String 1 blue size 6°, 3 green size 15°s, 2 purple size 11°s, 2 red size 11°s, and 2 pink size 11°s. Tie a square knot with the tail and working threads to form a circle. Pass through the first bead strung, making sure the knot doesn't slip inside the bead **(fig. 12, blue)**.

**ROUND 3** String 3 green size 15°s and 1 purple size 11°, skip the 3 green size 15°s of the starting ring, and pass through the next bead. String 1 red size 11°, skip 1 bead previously strung, and pass through the next bead. String 1 pink size 11°, skip 1 bead previously strung, and pass through the next bead. String 1 blue size 6°, skip 1 bead previously strung, and pass through

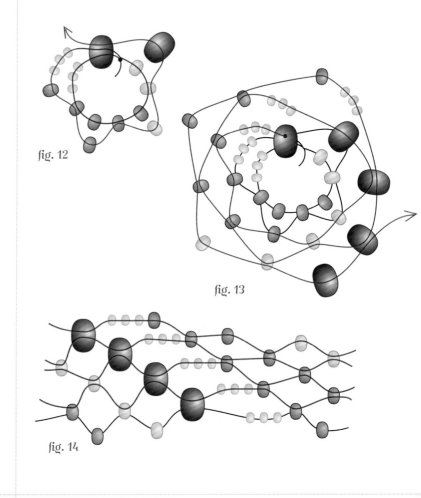

fig. 12

fig. 13

fig. 14

the next bead **(fig. 12, red)**. **note:** *No step up is required.*

**ROUNDS 4 AND ON** Work tubular peyote with 3 green size 15°s and 1 purple size 11° in the first stitch. (Remember to skip the previous green 15°s and pass only through the previous purple size 11°.) Work 1 red size 11° in the second stitch. Work 1 pink size 11° in the third stitch. Work

1 blue size 6° in the fourth stitch. Repeat the entire sequence to continue building the spiral. Here's another way to look at it: Always string a bead identical to the one you are about to enter in the previous round and continue to add 3 green size 15°s before stringing each purple bead. Work with relaxed tension so the work doesn't become too stiff, but not

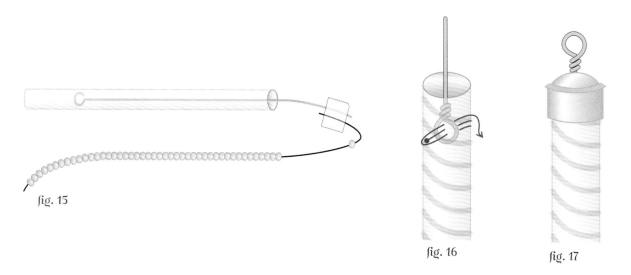

fig. 15

fig. 16

fig. 17

so relaxed that any stitches are left loose *(figs. 13 and 14)*.

## finishing beaded ropes

### core of beads

To give your beaded rope more structure, add a strand of beads to the inside: Before stitching the end of the tube closed, use beading wire or durable braided beading thread to string enough same-colored beads to match the length of your rope. Make sure the beads are small enough to fit inside the rope's core.

To help guide the strand of beads through the center of the rope, use a piece of gauged scrap wire that is longer than your tube as a makeshift needle: Use round-nose pliers to form a small simple or wrapped loop on one end of the gauged wire and

tape the end of the loaded beading wire (or thread) to the other end of the gauged wire. Make sure the loop of the wire can pass through the circle formed by the rope's starting round(s). Pass the round end of the gauged wire through the tube, pushing the beadwork down over the strand of beads. Once stringing is complete, work decreases at the end of the rope to enclose the strand of beads *(fig. 15)*.

### ends

To add a clean finish to the ends of your tubular-peyote rope, form a small wrapped loop at the end of 4" (10.2 cm) of 20-, 22-, or 24-gauge wire. Insert the loop into the end of the rope and securely stitch the loop to the rope, passing back and forth between the sides of the rope.

Secure the rope's thread and trim *(fig. 16)*.

Use the wire end to string 1 bead cap or cone (wide end first) down over the end of the tube and form a wrapped loop *(fig. 17)*. Attach your clasp or other design elements directly to this loop.

In this wonderfully decorative cuff that's teeming with rich colors and a tasteful mix of textures, Sherry shows us why tubular peyote is the perfect stitch for securing cabochons to a beading foundation. Her use of traditional stringing materials such as pressed-glass rectangles is inspiring; bead around them to show off their beautiful surfaces. ● *by sherry serafini*

# marcella cuff

**TECHNIQUES**

Tubular peyote stitch

Backstitch bead embroidery

Brick-stitch edging

Fringe

**MATERIALS**

1 g silver-lined teal matte AB size 15° beads (A)

1 g dark gold size 15° seed beads (B)

3 g dark gold size 11° seed beads (C)

3 g black size 11° seed beads (D)

1 g green 24k gold iris size 11° cylinder beads (E)

2 g heather gold matte metallic iris size 11° cylinder beads (F)

6 jet 2XAB 5mm crystal sequins

2 purple iris 6mm fire-polished rounds

4 turquoise/brown mottled 8×12mm pressed-glass rectangles

2 turquoise/brown mottled 11×18mm pressed-glass rectangles

8 lime green 3×5mm vertically drilled potato pearls

75–85 turquoise 3mm rounds

2 olive green 14mm acrylic cabochons

1 purple 18×25mm acrylic cabochon

1 copper 6×20mm 3-strand magnetic tube clasp

2" × 7" (5.1 × 17.8 cm) piece of beading foundation

2" × 7" (5.1 × 17.8 cm) piece of black Ultrasuede

Smoke 6 lb braided beading thread

Clear jeweler's adhesive

White tacky glue

**TOOLS**

Permanent marker

Toothpick

Scissors

Size 13 beading needle

**FINISHED SIZE**

2" × 6¾" (5.1 × 17.1 cm)

## 1 base.
**base.** Prepare the beading foundation and glue the cabochons in place:

**FOUNDATION** Using the permanent marker, mark the vertical and horizontal centerlines of the beading foundation. Draw a vertical line at each end so that the space between the lines equals your desired finished length, less ⅝" (1.6 cm) for the clasp. Don't trim the foundation.

**CABOCHONS** Spread clear adhesive on the back of the purple cabochon using a toothpick and center it on the beading foundation. Glue 1 olive cabochon on each side of the purple cabochon, centering them along the horizontal centerline and leaving ⅜" (1 cm) between each cabochon. Let dry for at least twenty minutes. Don't let any adhesive seep out around the edges of the cabochons.

## 2 center bezel.
**center bezel.** Use backstitch and tubular peyote stitch to bezel the purple cabochon:

**ROUNDS 1 AND 2** Tie a couple of strong overhand knots at the end of 3' (.9 m) of thread and place a needle at the other end. Pass through the foundation from back to front near the cabochon. String 2E, slide them to the backing, and lay them alongside the cabochon. Pass down through the foundation next to the last bead added. Pass up through the foundation before

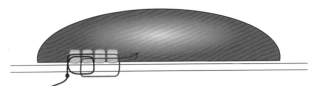

fig. 01: working the first two stitches of rounds 1 and 2

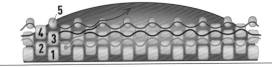

fig. 02: stitching rounds 3–5

fig. 03: backstitching with the turquoise rounds

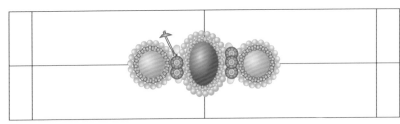

fig. 04: adding pearls and sequins

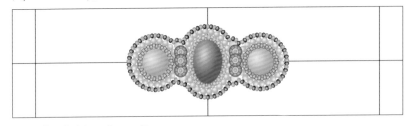

fig. 05: stitching the outline

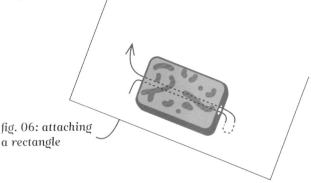

fig. 06: attaching a rectangle

the first bead added, then pass through the first and second beads *(fig. 01, blue)*. *String 2E, lay them alongside the purple cabochon, pass down through the foundation next to the last bead strung, pass up between the first and second beads, then pass through the last 3 beads *(fig. 01, red)*. Repeat from * to add a total of 52E or enough to surround the purple cabochon, making sure to add an even number of beads. note: *This circle of beads forms both Rounds 1 and 2 of the bezel.*

**ROUND 3** String 1E, skip the nearest backstitched E, and pass through the next E; repeat to add a total of 26E. Step up for each new round by passing through the first bead added in the current round *(fig. 02, green)*. note: *If you didn't use 52E for Rounds 1 and 2, adjust the number of beads in this and following rounds as needed by continuing to add 1 bead in each stitch.*

**ROUND 4** Work tubular peyote stitch with 1E in each stitch to add a total of 26E *(fig. 02, blue)*.

**ROUND 5** Work tubular peyote stitch with 1A in each stitch to add a total of 26A *(fig. 02, red)*. Repeat the thread path to reinforce, using tight tension to cause the beadwork to cup. Weave through beads to exit down through the foundation. Pass up through the foundation about 1.5mm (or equal to half the width of 1 turquoise round) outside of Round 1.

**ROUND 6** Adding 1 turquoise round at a time, backstitch around the bezel formed in Rounds 1–5 to add a total of 29 turquoise rounds or enough to surround the bezel *(fig. 03)*. Weave through beads to exit down through the foundation. Pass up through the foundation next to 1 olive cabochon.

**3 olive cabochons.** Use backstitch and tubular peyote stitch to bezel the olive cabochons:
**CABOCHONS** Repeat Step 2, using 38F for Rounds 1 and 2 (or enough to surround 1 olive cabochon), 19F in each of Rounds 3 and 4, 19B in Round 5, and 21–22 turquoise rounds in Round 6. Repeat this entire section to bezel the other olive cabochon.

**PEARLS** Backstitch 1 pearl in each corner where the turquoise rounds that surround the olive cabochons meet the turquoise rounds of the purple cabochon to add a total of 4 pearls *(fig. 04, green pearls)*.

**SEQUINS** Exiting in the "seam" between 1 olive cabochon and the purple cabochon, and between the pearls just added, string 1 sequin (back to front) and 1B; pass back through the sequin and through the beading foundation to form a fringe. Repeat the thread path to reinforce. Repeat to add 2 more fringes, filling the seam. Add 3 matching fringes between the other olive cabochon and the opposite side of the purple cabochon *(fig. 04, sequins)*.

**GOLD-AND-BLACK OUTLINE** Alternating 1C and 1D, backstitch around the outside edge of all the beads added so far *(fig. 05)*. Secure the thread and trim.

**4 rectangles.** Glue the rectangles in place and outline them with backstitch:
**ADHERE** Leaving enough room to outline each bead in size 11°s, use clear adhesive to adhere 1 large and 2 small rectangles on each end of the beading foundation, centered along the horizontal centerline (see *fig. 07* on page 78 for placement). Let dry at least 20 minutes. Start 3' (.9 m) of new thread that exits up through the foundation next to the hole in

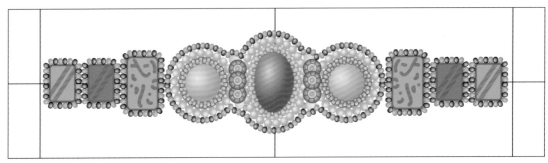

*fig. 07: outlining the rectangles*

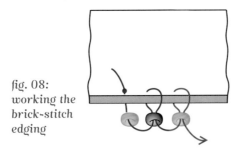

*fig. 08: working the brick-stitch edging*

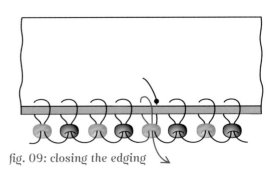

*fig. 09: closing the edging*

1 rectangle. Stitch each rectangle down to secure *(fig. 06)*. note: *Make sure you glue and stitch the rectangles securely since they are not bezeled in place.*

**OUTLINE** Alternating 1C and 1D, backstitch around each rectangle *(fig. 07)*. If needed, add more rectangles and/or rows of outline beads to reach the vertical end lines marked in Step 1. Secure the thread and trim.

**5** **finishing.** Add the backing, embellishment, brick-stitch edging, and clasp:

**BACKING** Carefully trim any excess foundation away from the beadwork, taking care to avoid cutting stitches. Use a toothpick to spread a thin, even layer of white glue to the back of the beadwork and press it onto the piece of Ultrasuede. Don't let any glue seep out around the edges of the foundation. Let dry for at least twenty minutes. Carefully trim the excess Ultrasuede flush with the beadwork.

**BRICK-STITCH EDGING** Tie a knot at the end of 2' (.6 m) of thread. Sew into the beadwork's edge from front to back to anchor the thread and hide the knot between beads. String 1C and 1D, lay the beads down along the edge of the work, and pass up through the edge of the Ultrasuede, the foundation, and back through the D just added; pull snug *(fig. 08, blue)*. String 1C, pass up through the edge of the Ultrasuede, the foundation, and back through

the C just added *(fig. 08, red)*; repeat along the entire edge of the beadwork, alternating 1C and 1D. Stitch through the first C added to close the edging *(fig. 09)*. note: *Adjust the spacing of the final few stitches so that the last bead added in the round is a D. Secure the thread and trim.*

**ADD THE CLASP** Tie a knot at the end of 2' (.6 m) of thread. Center the closed clasp along one end of the bracelet to find the proper placement. Sew into the beadwork's edge from front to back, hiding the knot between beads, and exit an edge bead near 1 of the clasp loops. String 2D, pass through the nearest clasp loop, string 2D; and pass back through the last bead exited on the bracelet. Repeat the thread path to reinforce. Weave through beads and the Ultrasuede/foundation layer to exit a bead near the next clasp loop. Attach each clasp loop to an edge bead in the same manner *(fig. 10)*. Repeat this entire section at the opposite end of the bracelet to attach the other side of the clasp, making sure the clasp is oriented so it will close properly. Secure the thread and trim.

**EMBELLISHMENT LOOPS** Center the needle on 12" (.3 m) of thread and tie a knot to create a doubled thread. Sew into the beadwork's edge from front to back, hiding the knot between beads, at the upper left-hand side of the purple cabochon, exiting from an edge bead. String 1C, 1 turquoise round, 1C, 1 pearl, 1 fire-polished round, 1 pearl, 1C, 1 turquoise round, and 1C; pass through the corresponding edge bead on the upper right side of the purple cabochon and beading foundation. Stitch through the beading foundation and Ultrasuede to exit back through the last edge bead entered and repeat the thread path to reinforce *(fig. 11)*. Repeat this entire section on the opposite side of the purple cabochon. Secure the threads and trim.

## TIPS

● Use fabric dye to color the beading foundation gray before stitching. This way the white of the foundation won't show through if you happen to leave space between stitches.

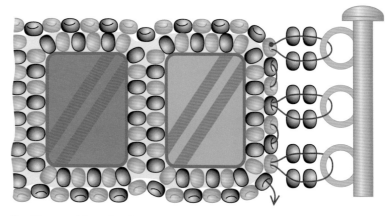

fig. 10: *attaching the clasp*

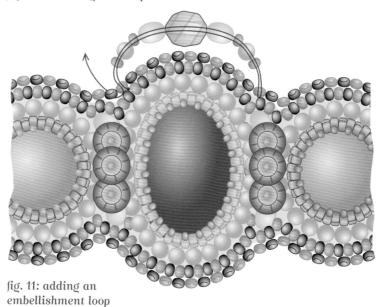

fig. 11: *adding an embellishment loop*

● If your cabochons are shorter or taller than the ones used here, adjust the number of rounds worked in each bezel as needed to secure them to the foundation. If a cabochon ever feels loose, work one or two more inside rounds using size 15° seed beads.

● Any bead that's flat on at least one side can be used in place of cabochons in bead-embroidered projects. Give these clever replacements a faux bezel by beading a border around them, as Sherry did with the flat rectangles in this design, instead of working a full bezel.

● See more embellishment and finishing ideas starting on page 139.

Every beader should know how to stitch three-dimensional shapes such as these circles, triangles, and squares. Not only do these shapes make great components for any design, but they are perfect for toggle clasps. Start with a circle and then see how a few herringbone stitches can transform a ring of beads into triangles and squares. • *by melinda barta*

# geometry 101

**TECHNIQUES**
Tubular and flat peyote stitch

Herringbone stitch

Zipping

**FINISHED SIZE**
7" (17.8 cm)

# CIRCLES

## MATERIALS

3 g green teal matte metallic iris size 15°
Japanese seed beads (A)

5 g gray mist matte metallic size 15°
Japanese seed beads (B)

6 g green teal matte metallic iris size 11°
Japanese seed beads (C)

.5 g seafoam green–lined amber size 11°
Japanese seed beads (D)

2 clear with teal stripe matte 25mm with
4mm hole lampwork discs

Smoke 6 lb braided beading thread

## TOOLS

Size 10 and 12 beading needles

Scissors or thread burner

**1** Use tubular peyote stitch to
form a circle by stitching 2 sides
off a central ring and zipping the sides
together along the outside edge:

**ROUNDS 1 AND 2** Use 5' (1.5 m) of
thread to string 40A, leaving a
6" (15.2 cm) tail. Tie a square knot
with the tail and working threads
to form a ring, leaving one bead's
width of space so the ring is not
too tight. Pass through the first
bead strung, making sure the
knot doesn't slip inside the bead
*(fig. 01)*.

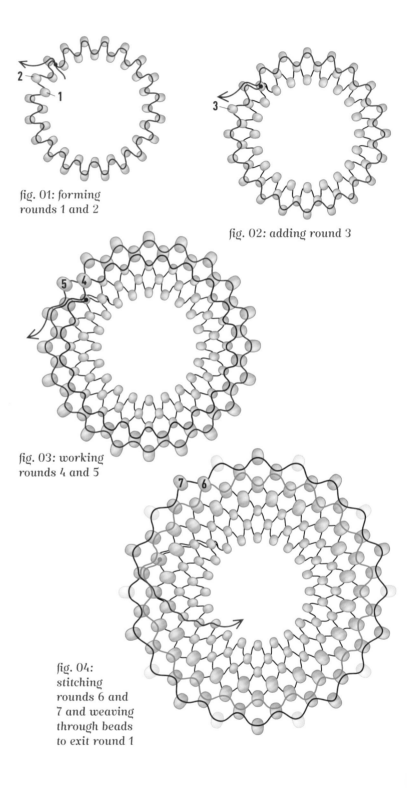

fig. 01: forming
rounds 1 and 2

fig. 02: adding round 3

fig. 03: working
rounds 4 and 5

fig. 04:
stitching
rounds 6 and
7 and weaving
through beads
to exit round 1

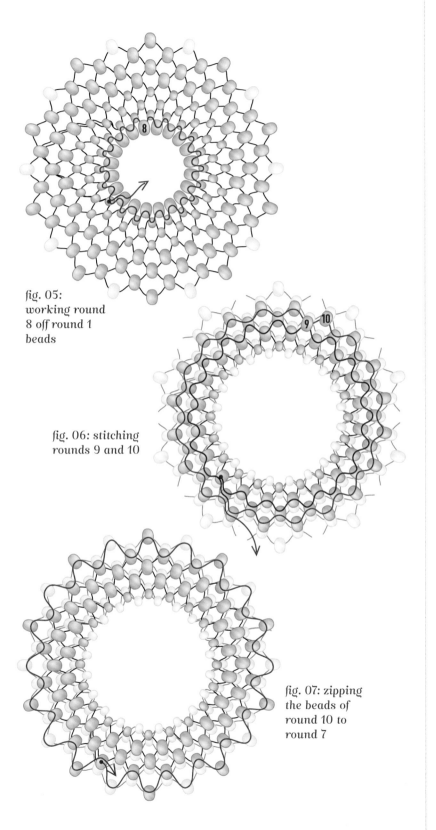

fig. 05:
working round
8 off round 1
beads

fig. 06: stitching
rounds 9 and 10

fig. 07: zipping
the beads of
round 10 to
round 7

**ROUND 3** String 1A, skip 1A previously strung, and pass through the next A; repeat nineteen times to add a total of 20A. **note:** *Step up for each new round by passing through the first bead added in the current round **(fig. 02)**. To keep the beadwork flexible, use relaxed thread tension.*

**ROUND 4** Work 1C in each stitch to add a total of 20C **(fig. 03, blue)**.

**ROUND 5** Repeat Round 4 **(fig. 03, red)**.

**ROUND 6** Repeat Round 4 **(fig. 04, green)**. **note:** *Work with slightly tighter thread tension in Rounds 6 and 7 so the beadwork cups.*

**ROUND 7** Work 1 stitch with 1D and 1 stitch with 1C; repeat this sequence nine times to add a total of 10D and 10C **(fig. 04, blue)**. Weave through beads to exit Round 1 **(fig. 04, red)**.

**ROUND 8** Work off Round 1 with 1C in each stitch to add a total of 20C **(fig. 05)**. Hold the beadwork so that the beads added for this second side are inside the cup of beadwork. As you work this side, manipulate the beads with your thumb and index finger to encourage the cupping of the beadwork. The sides will curl up toward each other.

**ROUND 9** Repeat Round 4 **(fig. 06, blue)**.

**ROUND 10** Repeat Round 4 **(fig. 06, red)**.

**ZIP** To double the working thread, move the needle closer to the beadwork so the end of the thread extends 5" (12.7 cm) beyond the last bead exited. Fold

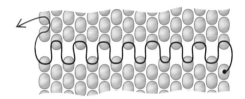

fig. 08: zipping the
toggle bar closed

fig. 09: embellishing the
end of the toggle bar

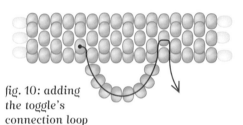

fig. 10: adding
the toggle's
connection loop

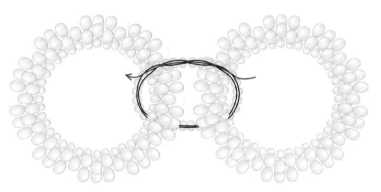

fig. 11: making a beaded ring

fig. 12: forming the clasp chain
and assembling the bracelet

the sides up toward each other
so that Round 7 meets Round
10 and zip the edges together
*(fig. 07)*. Secure the threads and
trim.

Repeat this entire step three
times for a total of 4 beaded circles.
Set the circles aside.

**2 toggle bar:** Make a strip
with flat peyote stitch, zip the
ends to form a tube, embellish the
ends, and add a connection loop:

**TUBE** Use 3' (.9 m) of thread and
C to work a strip 16 beads wide
and 10 rows long. Fold the ends
toward each other so Row 1
meets Row 10 and zip the edges
together *(fig. 08, blue)*. Weave
through beads to exit away from
the beadwork from 1 end C
*(fig. 08, red)*.

**END EMBELLISHMENT** String 1D,
pass down through the next
end C and up through the next;
repeat twice *(fig. 09)*. Repeat the
embellishment around the end of
the tube once more to add a total
of 5D. Weave through beads of
the tube or pass the needle down
through the center of the tube,
to exit an end C and repeat this
embellishment at the other end.

**CONNECTION LOOP** Weave through
beads to exit 5C from one end of
the tube. String 8C, pass through
1C in the row above the one just
exited, 5 beads in from the other
end *(fig. 10)*. Weave through
beads to work a turnaround and
reinforce the loop. Secure the
thread and trim.

**3 bracelet assembly.** Join the glass discs, beaded circles, and the clasp with simple seed bead rings:

**BEADED RINGS** Use 10" (25.4 cm) of thread to string 32B and 2 beaded circles, leaving a 4" (10.2 cm) tail. Pass through all the beads again and tie a square knot to form a tight circle. Pass through 3 beads, tie a knot, pass through 3 more beads, and trim the thread; add a needle to the tail thread and repeat **(fig. 11)**. Repeat to form a second 32B loop that joins the same 2 beaded circles. Form two 40B rings that join 1 of the previous beaded circles to 1 disc. Form two 40B rings that join the other side of this disc to 1 beaded circle. Form two 32B rings that join the previous beaded circle to the remaining beaded circle. Form two 40B rings that join the previous beaded circle to the remaining disc. Form two 34B rings that connect to the last disc.

**TOGGLE CHAIN** *Form one 14C ring that attaches to both of the previous rings. Form two 20B rings that attach to the previous ring. Repeat from * twice more, or for the desired length, connecting the final pair of 20B rings to the toggle's connection loop **(fig. 12)**. note: *Work an even number of rings so the toggle aligns with the discs and beaded circles.*

## TRIANGLES

### MATERIALS
5 g gray lichen matte metallic iris size 11° Japanese seed beads (A)

6 g olive-gold matte metallic size 11° Japanese seed beads (B)

.5 g seafoam green–lined amber size 11° Japanese seed beads (C)

3 frosted green 26mm recycled glass rings

Smoke 6 lb braided beading thread

### TOOLS
Size 10 and 12 beading needles

Scissors or thread burner

**1** Use tubular peyote stitch and herringbone stitch to form a triangle by stitching 2 sides off a central ring and zipping the sides together along the outside edge:

**ROUNDS 1 AND 2** Use 5' (1.5 m) of thread to string 36A, leaving a 6" (15.2 cm) tail. Tie a square knot with the tail and working threads to form a ring, leaving 1 bead's width of space so the ring is not too tight. Pass through the first bead strung, making sure the knot doesn't slip inside the bead **(fig. 01)**.

**ROUND 3** String 2A, skip 1A previously strung, and pass through the next A. String 1A, skip 1A previously strung, and pass through the next A; repeat four times. Repeat the entire sequence twice to add a total of 21A. **note:** *Step up for each new round by passing through the first bead added in the current round **(fig. 02)**. To keep the beadwork flexible, use relaxed thread tension.*

**ROUND 4** String 2A; pass through the next A of Round 3 (without skipping over a bead). **note:** *This forms the first herringbone stitch.* Work 6 tubular peyote stitches with 1A in each stitch. Repeat the

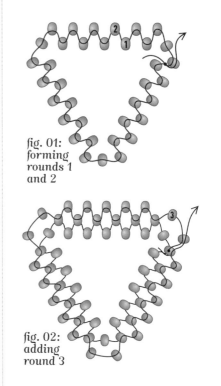

fig. 01: forming rounds 1 and 2

fig. 02: adding round 3

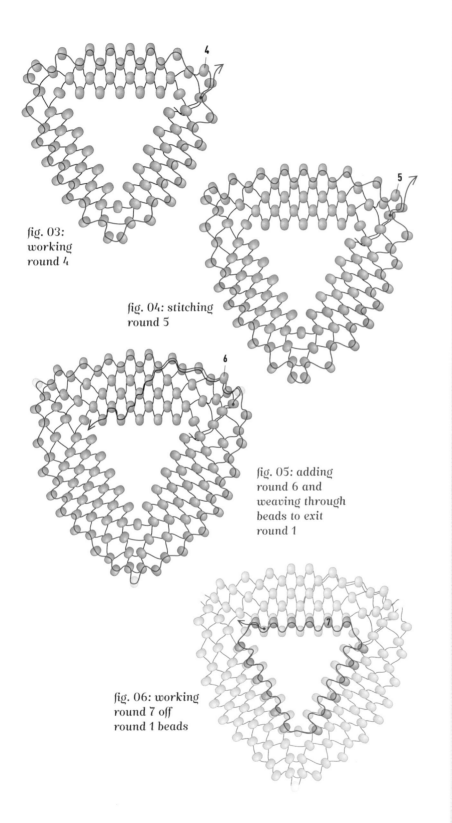

fig. 03:
working
round 4

fig. 04: stitching
round 5

fig. 05: adding
round 6 and
weaving through
beads to exit
round 1

fig. 06: working
round 7 off
round 1 beads

entire sequence twice to add a
total of 24A *(fig. 03)*.

**ROUND 5** String 2A; pass through
the next A of Round 4 (without
skipping over a bead). Work
7 tubular peyote stitches with 1A
in each stitch. Repeat the entire
sequence twice to add a total of
27A *(fig. 04)*.

**ROUND 6** String 1C; pass through
the next A of Round 5 to add a
bead at the tip of the herringbone
column. Work 8 tubular peyote
stitches with 1A in each stitch.
Repeat the entire sequence twice
to add a total of 24A and 3C
*(fig. 05, blue)*. Weave through
beads to exit toward a corner in
Round 1 *(fig. 05, red)*.

**ROUND 7** Work tubular peyote
stitch off Round 1 with 1A in
each stitch to add a total of 18A
*(fig. 06)*. Hold the beadwork
so that the beads added for
this second side are inside the
triangle of beadwork. As you
work this side, manipulate the
beads with your thumb and index
finger to encourage the second
side to begin folding up over the
first side.

**ROUND 8** String 2A; pass through
the next A of Round 7 (without
skipping over a bead). Work
5 tubular peyote stitches with 1A
in each stitch. Repeat the entire
sequence twice to add a total of
21A *(fig. 07)*.

**ROUND 9** String 2A; pass through
the next A of Round 8 (without
skipping over a bead). Work
6 tubular peyote stitches with
1A in each stitch. Repeat the

entire sequence twice to add a total of 24A *(fig. 08, blue)*.

**ROUND 10** String 2A; pass through the next A of Round 9 (without skipping over a bead). Work 7 tubular peyote stitches with 1A in each stitch. Repeat the entire sequence twice to add a total of 27A *(fig. 08, red)*.

**ZIP** To double the working thread, move the needle closer to the beadwork so the end of the thread extends 5" (12.7 cm) beyond the last bead exited. Fold the sides up toward each other so that Round 6 meets Round 10 and zip the edges together *(fig. 09)*. Secure the threads and trim.

Repeat this entire step twice using B in place of A for a total of 2 olive beaded triangles. Set the triangles aside.

**2** *toggle bar:* Make a strip with flat peyote stitch, zip the ends to form a tube, embellish the ends, and add a connection loop:

**TUBE** Use 3' (.9 m) of thread and A to work a strip 16 beads wide and 12 rows long. Fold the ends toward each other so Row 1 meets Row 12 and zip the edges together. Weave through beads to exit away from the beadwork from 1 end A.

**END EMBELLISHMENT** String 1C, pass down through the next end A to the right, and up through the following end A *(fig. 10, blue)*; repeat twice. String 1C; pass down through the nearest end A to the left to reverse directions and up through the following

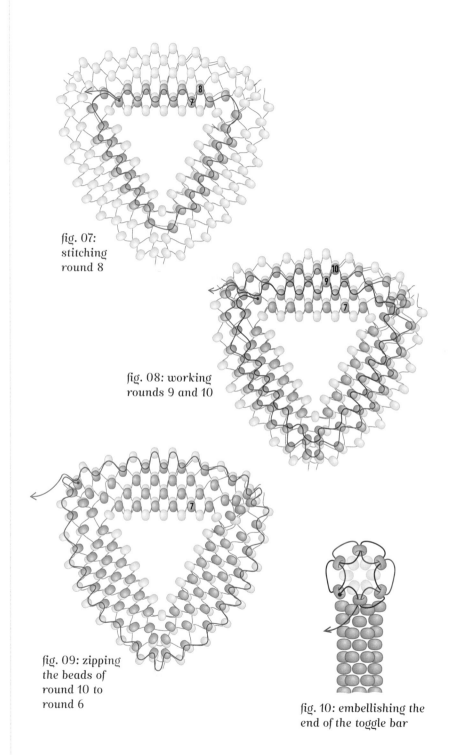

fig. 07: stitching round 8

fig. 08: working rounds 9 and 10

fig. 09: zipping the beads of round 10 to round 6

fig. 10: embellishing the end of the toggle bar

end A. String 1C; pass down through the next end A to the left and up through the following end A. String 1C; pass down through the next end A to the left **(fig. 10, red)** to add a total of 6C. Weave through beads of the tube or pass the needle down through the center of the tube, to exit an end A and repeat this embellishment at the other end.

**CONNECTION LOOP** Repeat Circles, Step 2, Connection Loop using 8A.

# 3 bracelet assembly.

Join the glass rings, beaded triangles, and the clasp with simple seed bead rings:

**BEADED RINGS** Forming the rings as in Circles, Step 3, make two 26A rings that join 1 olive triangle to 1 glass ring. Form two 32B rings that join the previous glass ring to 1 gray triangle. Form two 32B rings that join the previous triangle to 1 glass ring. Form two 26A rings that join the previous glass ring to the remaining olive triangle. Form two 26A rings that connect the previous triangle to the remaining glass ring. Form two 22B rings that attach to the last glass ring. **note:** *Because size 11° seed beads can vary from one tube to the next, you may need to adjust the number of beads used for the beaded rings. Just make sure the triangles have room to move around inside the beaded rings.*

**TOGGLE CHAIN** Form one 15A ring that attaches to both of the previous rings. Form one 14B ring that joins the previous ring to the toggle's connection loop. **note:** *If adjusting the length of the chain, work an even number of rings so the toggle aligns with the glass rings and triangles.*

## SQUARES

### MATERIALS

9 g red purple matte metallic iris size 11° Japanese seed beads (A)

.5 g seafoam green–lined amber size 11° Japanese seed beads (B)

4 g cranberry/purple/olive/navy striped matte size 11° Czech seed beads (C)

2 clear with red-and-purple stripes matte 23mm lampwork rings

Smoke 6 lb braided beading thread

### TOOLS

Size 10 and 12 beading needles

Scissors or thread burner

**1** Use tubular peyote stitch and herringbone stitch to form a square by stitching 2 sides off a central ring and zipping the sides together along the outside edge:

**ROUNDS 1 AND 2** Use 5' (1.5 m) of thread to string 32A, leaving a 6" (15.2 cm) tail. Tie a square knot with the tail and working threads to form a ring, leaving 1 bead's width of space so the ring is not too tight. Pass through the first bead strung, making sure the knot doesn't slip inside the bead **(fig. 01)**.

**ROUND 3** String 2A, skip 1A previously strung, and pass through the next A. String 1A, skip 1A previously strung, and pass through the next A; repeat twice. Repeat the entire sequence three times to add a total of

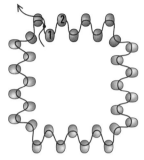

fig. 01: forming
rounds 1 and 2

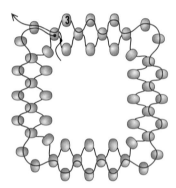

fig. 02: adding round 3

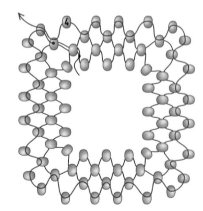

fig. 03: working round 4

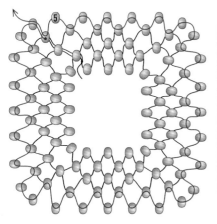

fig. 04: stitching
round 5

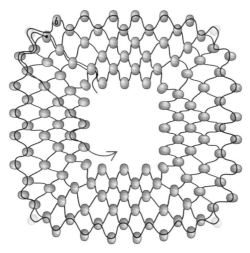

fig. 05: adding
round 6 and
weaving
through beads
to exit round 1

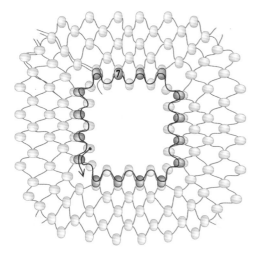

fig. 06:
working
round 7 off
round 1 beads

20A. note: *Step up for each new round by passing through the first bead added in the current round (fig. 02). To keep the beadwork flexible, use relaxed thread tension.*

**ROUND 4** String 2A; pass through the next A of Round 3 (without skipping over a bead). note: *This forms the first herringbone stitch.* Work 4 tubular peyote stitches with 1A in each stitch. Repeat the entire sequence three times to add a total of 24A *(fig. 03)*.

**ROUND 5** String 2A; pass through the next A of Round 4 (without skipping over a bead). Work 5 tubular peyote stitches with 1A in each stitch. Repeat the entire sequence three times to add a total of 28A *(fig. 04)*.

**ROUND 6** String 1C; pass through the next A of Round 5 to add a bead at the tip of the herringbone column. Work 6 tubular peyote stitches with 1A in each stitch. Repeat the entire sequence three times to add a total of 24A and 4C *(fig. 05, blue)*. Weave through beads to exit toward a corner in Round 1 *(fig. 05, red)*.

**ROUND 7** Work tubular peyote stitch off Round 1 with 1A in each stitch to add a total of 16A *(fig. 06)*. Hold the beadwork so that the beads added for this second side are inside the square of beadwork. As you work this side, manipulate the beads with your thumb and index finger to encourage the second side to begin folding up over the first side.

**ROUND 8** String 2A; pass through the next A of Round 7 (without

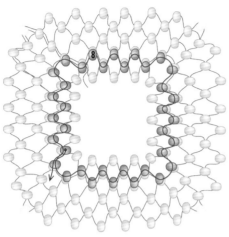

fig. 07: stitching
round 8

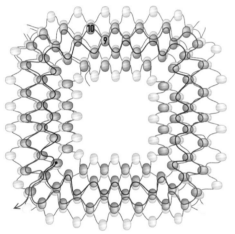

fig. 08: working
rounds 9 and 10

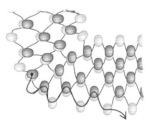

fig. 09: zipping the beads
of round 10 to round 6

skipping over a bead). Work 3 tubular peyote stitches with 1A in each stitch. Repeat the entire sequence three times to add a total of 20A *(fig. 07)*.

**ROUND 9** String 2A; pass through the next A of Round 8 (without skipping over a bead). Work 4 tubular peyote stitches with 1A in each stitch. Repeat the entire sequence three times to add a total of 24A *(fig. 08, blue)*.

**ROUND 10** String 2A; pass through the next A of Round 9 (without skipping over a bead). Work 5 tubular peyote stitches with 1A in each stitch. Repeat the entire sequence three times to add a total of 28A *(fig. 08, red)*.

**ZIP** To double the working thread, move the needle closer to the beadwork so the end of the thread extends 5" (12.7 cm) beyond the last bead exited. Fold the sides up toward each other so that Round 6 meets Round 10 and zip the edges together *(fig. 09)*. Secure the threads and trim. Repeat this entire step twice for a total of 3 beaded squares. Set the squares aside.

**2** **toggle bar.** Repeat Circles, Step 2, using A for the toggle bar and connection loop and B for the end embellishment.

**3** **bracelet assembly.** Join glass rings, beaded squares, and the clasp with simple seed bead rings:
**BEADED RINGS** Forming the rings as in Circles, Step 3, make one

28C ring. Form two 16A rings that attach to the previous ring. Form one 28C ring that attaches to both of the previous rings. Form two 20C rings that join the previous ring to 1 beaded square. *Form two 27C rings that join the previous square to 1 lampwork ring. Form two 27C rings that join the previous lampwork ring to 1 beaded square. Repeat from *.

**TOGGLE CHAIN** Form two 20C rings that attach to the previous beaded square. Form one 14A ring that attaches to both of the previous rings. Form one 14C ring that joins the previous ring to the toggle's connection loop. **note:** *Adjust the length by adding or subtracting loops in multiples of 2 before adding the toggle, or at the starting end of the bracelet.*

## TIPS

● When working herringbone-stitch corners, be sure the corners "click" into place and the 2 beads angle away from each other.

● It's important to cull inconsistently sized beads when working dimensional rings; otherwise, the components can become misshapen. Odd-shaped beads used for the herringbone stitches in the triangles and squares can skew the corners or create unwanted tight spots that lead to breakage.

● For minor bracelet size adjustments, change the number of beads in the rings that join the components. For more drastic size adjustments, add or subtract components. If adjusting the length of the chain near the toggle, make sure it remains long enough for the toggle bar to pass through the clasp ring.

● You may find it helpful to work the herringbone-stitch beads in a different color to differentiate them from the peyote-stitch side beads.

● If the beaded tube that serves as the toggle bar bends, insert a short piece of 18-gauge (or thicker) wire or a trimmed toothpick into the tube. Add more embellishments at the ends to hold the wire/toothpick in place, or use a little bit of clear jeweler's cement such as E-6000.

● If you don't like how the shapes can rotate once the bracelet is assembled, stitch the beaded connection rings to the shapes.

● Count out the number of beads needed for each round so you know you've added the correct amount before moving on to the next round.

● When working the triangles and squares, it's always easiest to start the next round with a herringbone stitch. If you start a new round on one of the peyote sides, you'll need to work a step up at the end of each round. Plus, since the peyote step ups will constantly shift in subsequent rounds, the pattern won't be as easy to follow.

## DESIGN OPTIONS

● This bracelet (right) is a great example of how rings can be used both as design elements and as a toggle ring. Experiment with pattern by joining the rings with decorative flat peyote–stitch bands edged with picots. The toggle bar is wrapped with a flat peyote–stitch band for a fun variation.

● The peyote rings in this quirky combination (left) of pewter findings and seed beads were given 3-bead picots along the outside edge to mimic the border of the Green Girl Studios "sun rock" rings. The picots were randomly worked off Rounds 6, 7, and 10. Beaded rings join the components and a matching pewter clasp.

I've used tubular peyote circles in my designs for years and one day started to wonder if I could easily turn the shape into an oval. A simple mix of size 15° and 11° beads in the starting rounds did the trick. This design would look great in any color combination, not just the sunny, happy shades used here. ● *by melinda barta*

# happy-go-lucky links

### TECHNIQUES
Tubular, flat, and circular peyote stitch

Zipping

### MATERIALS
4 g mint-lined gold size 15° Japanese seed beads (A)

11 g sage gray-lined topaz size 11° Japanese seed beads (B)

18 g bronze-lined light aqua AB size 11° Japanese seed beads (C)

9 g deep turquoise-lined amber size 11° Japanese seed beads (D)

8 g blue/lavender luster iris size 11° Japanese seed beads (E)

14 seafoam-lined light topaz AB size 8° Japanese seed beads (F)

7 orange swirl with multicolored circles and dots 20×16×15mm lampwork ovals (G)

Smoke 6 lb braided beading thread

### TOOLS
Scissors or thread burner

Size 10 or 12 beading needle

### FINISHED SIZE
33¼" (84.5 cm)

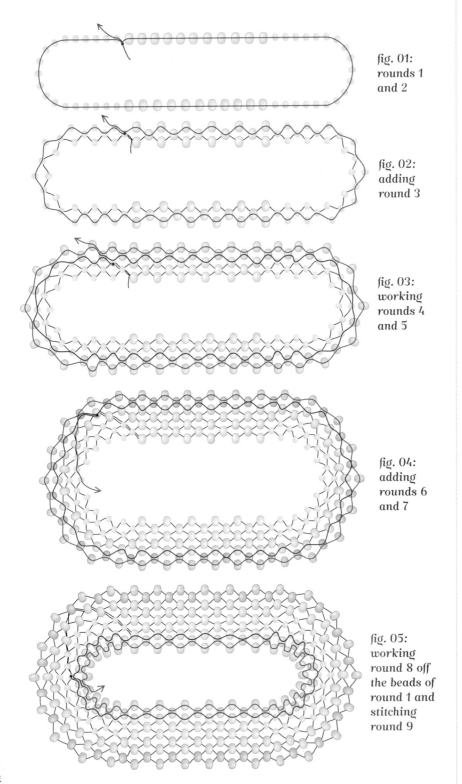

fig. 01:
rounds 1
and 2

fig. 02:
adding
round 3

fig. 03:
working
rounds 4
and 5

fig. 04:
adding
rounds 6
and 7

fig. 05:
working
round 8 off
the beads of
round 1 and
stitching
round 9

**1 oval ring.** Use tubular peyote stitch to form an oval beaded ring by stitching 2 sides off a central ring and then zipping the sides together along the outside edge. **note on tension:** *It's important to use relaxed tension when stitching the oval rings. If you pull each stitch too snug, the rings can get tight, and, if you squeeze one when tight, the beads can break. If you naturally bead with tight tension, think of relaxing your hands as you stitch. Of course, you don't want thread showing or beads sagging, but don't tug on the thread after each bead is added. In Rounds 6 and 7, the beadwork will begin to cup, so use enough tension to encourage the shape. (If you don't, you'll have a lot of thread showing between beads, so naturally you'll want to pull the beads into a cupped shape anyway.) The size difference between the size 15° seed beads and the size 11° seed beads—not the use of tight tension—makes the beadwork curve on the ends.*

Start with the size 10 needle and switch to the size 12 if you ever have trouble fitting the needle through beads.

**ROUNDS 1 AND 2** Use 6' (1.8 m) of thread to string 19A, 11B, 19A, and 11B. Leaving a 3–4" (7.6–10.2 cm) tail and 1 or 2 bead's width of space within the circle, tie a square knot with the tail and working threads to form a circle. Pass through the first A strung, making sure the knot doesn't slip inside the bead **(fig. 01)**.

**ROUND 3** *String 1A, skip 1A previously strung, and pass through the next A; repeat eight times to add a total of 9A. String

1B, skip 1B previously strung, and pass through the next bead; repeat five times to add a total of 6B. Repeat from * *(fig. 02)*. **note:** Step up for each new round by passing through the first bead added in the current round. Make sure the work doesn't twist.

**ROUND 4** Work 1C in each stitch to add a total of 30C *(fig. 03, blue)*.

**ROUND 5** Repeat Round 4 *(fig. 03, red)*.

**ROUND 6** Work 1D in each stitch to add a total of 30D *(fig. 04, blue)*. **note:** *Work with slightly tighter thread tension in Rounds 6 and 7 so the beadwork cups.*

**ROUND 7** Work 1E in each stitch to add a total of 30E. Weave through beads to exit Round 1 *(fig. 04, red)*.

**ROUND 8** Work off Round 1 with 1C in each stitch to add a total of 30C *(fig. 05, blue)*. Hold the beadwork so that the beads added in this and subsequent rounds are inside of the cup of beadwork. As you work this second side of the ring, manipulate the beads with your thumb and index finger to encourage the cupping of the beadwork. The sides curl up toward each other.

**ROUND 9** Work 1C in each stitch to add a total of 30C *(fig. 05, red)*.

**ROUND 10** Work 1D in each stitch to add a total of 30D.

**ZIP** To double the working thread, move the needle closer to the beadwork so the tail thread extends 5" (12.7 cm) beyond the last bead exited. Fold the sides of the beadwork up toward each other so that Round 7 meets

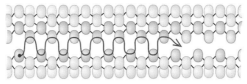

fig. 06: zipping rounds 7 and 10

fig. 07: stitching rounds 1–3 of the ring-to-ring connection

fig. 08: adding rounds 4 and 5

fig. 09: joining the ends of the connection strip

Round 10 and zip the edges together *(fig. 06)*. Repeat the thread path to reinforce. Secure the threads and trim.

Repeat this entire step sixteen times for a total of 17 beaded rings. Set the beaded rings aside.

## 2 ring-to-ring connections. Make a strip

of flat peyote stitch and connect the ends to join 2 beaded rings:

**ROWS 1 AND 2** Use 2' (.6 m) of thread to string 24B, leaving an 8" (20.3 cm) tail *(fig. 07, blue)*.

**ROW 3** String 1B, skip 1B previously strung, and pass through the next B; repeat eleven times to add a total of 12B *(fig. 07, red)*.

**ROW 4** Work 1E in each stitch to add a total of 12E. Pass back through the last bead of Row 1 *(fig. 08, blue)*.

**ROW 5** Work off Row 1 with 1E in each stitch to add a total of 11E *(fig. 07, red)*.

**JOIN** Wrap the strip around 2 beaded rings. String 1E and pass through the nearest beads of Rows 1 and 5 on the other end of the strip *(fig. 09)*. Pull tight to join the 2 ends of the beadwork.

**REINFORCE OUTSIDE ROWS** Weave through the next bead of Row 1,

fig. 10: connecting
the outside rows

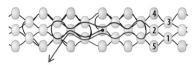

fig. 11: joining the inside rows

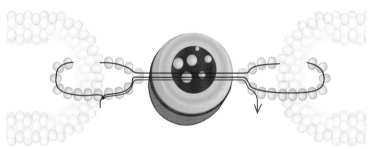

fig. 12: starting the beaded links

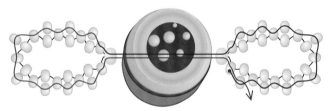

fig. 13: adding round 3 to the beaded link
[beaded rings removed for clarity]

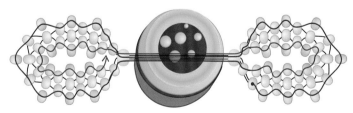

fig. 14: working rounds 4 and 5
[beaded rings removed for clarity]

the next bead of Row 5, and the next bead of Row 1. Work a turnaround by passing through the nearest beads of Rows 3 and 4. Follow the thread path of Row 4 back toward and across the join *(fig. 10, blue)*. Work a turnaround by passing through the nearest beads of Rows 1 and 5, then follow the thread path of Row 5 back toward and across the join *(fig. 10, red)*. Use tight thread tension to snug the ends of the peyote strip toward each other. Repeat the thread path to reinforce. Secure the thread and trim.

**REINFORCE INSIDE ROWS** Add a needle to the tail thread. Pass through the nearest bead of Row 1, the next bead of Row 2, and the next bead of Row 1. Work a turnaround to exit the nearest bead of Row 3. Follow the thread path of Row 3 back toward and across the join *(fig. 11, blue)*. Work a turnaround to exit the nearest bead of Row 1 and weave through the beads of Rows 1 and 2 back toward and across the join *(fig. 11, red)*. Use tight thread tension to snug the ends of the peyote strip toward each other. Repeat the thread path to reinforce. Secure the thread and trim.

Repeat this entire step nine times to make a chain of 11 beaded rings.

**3** **beaded links.** Use circular peyote stitch to form beaded links that join 2 beaded rings with 1 lampwork oval in the center:

**ROUNDS 1 AND 2** Use 30" (76.2 cm) of thread to string 3B, 1F, 1G, 1F, and 17B; pass through the center of 1 beaded ring at the end of the beaded-ring chain. Pass back through the F/G/F, leaving a 6" (15.2 cm) tail. String 14B; pass through the center of 1 beaded ring. Snug the beads and tie a square knot to form a circle *(fig. 12, blue)*. Pass through the first 3B, F/G/F, and 1B, making sure the knot doesn't slip inside a bead *(fig. 12, red)*. note: *If an F slips inside the hole in your lampwork oval, string as many are needed to ensure that 1F shows on each end of the oval. You will continue to pass from one side to the next as you build the links.*

**ROUND 3** String 1B, skip 1B previously strung, and pass through the next B; repeat seven times to add a total of 8B. Pass back through the F/G/F and next B *(fig. 13, blue)*. String 1B, skip 1B previously strung, and pass through the next B; repeat seven times to add a total of 8B. Weave through beads to exit the first bead added in this round *(fig. 13, red)*.

**ROUND 4** Work 1E in each stitch to add a total of 7E. Weave through the center beads to exit 1B of Round 1 or 3 on the other side of the G. note: *As the loops form it can be hard to distinguish between Rounds 1 and 3; either is fine to work on at this point.* Work 1E in each stitch to add a total of 7E. Weave through the center beads to exit the B of Round 1 nearest the B first exited in this round *(fig. 14, blue)*.

**ROUND 5** Work 1E in each stitch to add a total of 7E. Weave through the center beads to exit 1B of Round 1 or 3. note: *The beads worked in this round are opposite the round of E just added, so if you added Round 4 beads to Round 1, exit the B of Round 3; if you added Round 4 beads to Round 3, exit the B of Round 1.* Work 1E in each stitch to add a total of 7E *(fig. 14, red)*. Secure the threads and trim.

Repeat this entire step six times, forming links that attach 1 new beaded ring to the last beaded ring added. For the last link, join the final beaded ring to the free end of the beaded-ring chain. The necklace is long enough to slip over your head, so no clasp is needed.

## TIPS

● It is especially important to cull your beads when beading dimensional rings. Beads that are too thin or too wide can distort the overall shape or form tight spots that cause bead breakage. However, when working Round 4, using slightly thinner beads at the ends (between the size 15°s of the previous rounds) can be to your advantage; this will make the increase more gradual and help ensure smooth end curves.

● Add a clasp if shortening the length of the necklace.

● For a quicker project, consider making just the central part of the necklace (with beaded rings alternating with beaded links) and use metal chain for the back half of the necklace.

● The ring-to-ring connections can also be worked with circular peyote stitch. However, working them in flat peyote stitch and then joining the strip into a ring is a faster way to work.

## DESIGN OPTION

● To create an interesting chain of interlocking links, repeat Step 1 to make an oval as usual. For the following links, pass the strand of Round 1 and 2 beads through the opening in the previous oval before tying the square knot. Rotate the beadwork as needed to keep the previous oval out of your stitching path.

# peyote extras

Take your skills to the next level by trying your hand at freeform and sculptural peyote stitches. Then see how peyote is the perfect match for other stitches such as herringbone, right-angle weave, and netting.

Jean Campbell eases you into the wonderfully chaotic world of freeform peyote. The petals of her sweet **Daisy Girl** necklace start with a structured outline, and then she sets you free to fill in each petal as you see fit.

Sculptural peyote stitch is at its best in Jean Power's **Urban Skyline** necklace. Surprisingly easy to make, each triangular beaded bead in this showstopper is made three-dimensional by employing flat and tubular peyote stitches.

Switch from peyote to netting and back to peyote again in Cynthia Rutledge's crystal-studded **Pi R-Squared Lariat**. This combination of stitches enables you to embed sparkling bicone embellishments inside circle, square, and triangle focals.

The fun-to-stitch bead caps, used to accent beautiful pearls in my **Beaujolais** necklace, have tubular peyote–stitched walls and herringbone-stitched corners. This pattern demonstrates just how well these two stitches pair up.

See how right-angle-weave units are the perfect base for peyote stitch in my **On Broadway Beauties** bracelet-and-earring set. Plus, since one round of right-angle weave is as tall as several rounds of peyote stitch, you can cut down on a little beading time when starting your bezels.

*Take peyote to other dimensions, then see how effortlessly it pairs with other favorite stitches.*

## TECHNIQUES

### freeform peyote stitch

Instead of following a pattern bead by bead, stitch by stitch, freeform peyote stitch uses the skills you've learned thus far to create any shape of beadwork you desire. For example, build the body of a piece using a combination of one- and two-drop peyote stitches, work a series of increases or decreases, embed larger accent beads, or purposefully leave openings.

Don't hesitate to mix bead types and sizes, adjusting the number of beads used in each stitch to keep the beadwork tight *(fig. 01)*. The most successful freeform pieces leave no openings or gaps between beads (unless creating the intentional openings covered in Basics) and leave no thread showing—you still want the beadwork to be tight and strong.

### sculptural peyote

Any variation of peyote stitch can be used to create a three-dimensional work. Through a series of increases

and decreases, a change in bead type or size, a switch from one stitch variation to another, or the twisting and turning of a flat strip, any piece of beadwork that starts out flat can be manipulated into a sculptural form.

Some beaders use a small paintbrush to apply a thin coat of Pledge Premium Floor Finish with Future Shine (formerly sold as Future Floor Finish) to help their sculptural pieces hold shape. Some even dip their entire finished project in the floor polish, allowing it to drain and dry on a paper towel; this method is best for pieces that aren't intended to be worn.

When tight tension is important to maintaining the shape of the work, try using a waxed doubled thread. Filling the bead holes with several passes of thread will help stiffen the work.

### herringbone combinations
#### *shaping turns and corners*

A few herringbone stitches go a long way—they can be used to magically turn a circle of beadwork into other shapes including squares, rectangles, and triangles.

To begin adding herringbone stitches in the body of the bead-work, stitch a row/round with 1 bead in each stitch and add 2 beads in the stitch where you want to start the column of herringbone stitches *(fig.02)*.

When working the next row/round, string 2 beads after passing through the first bead of the previous pair. Pass through the next bead of the previous pair. This forms the first herringbone stitch. Continue working across the row/round with 1 bead in each stitch *(fig. 03)*.

Continue working herringbone stitches off the previous herring-

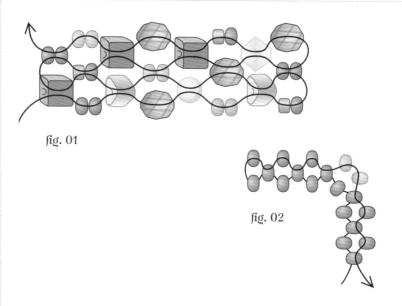

fig. 01

fig. 02

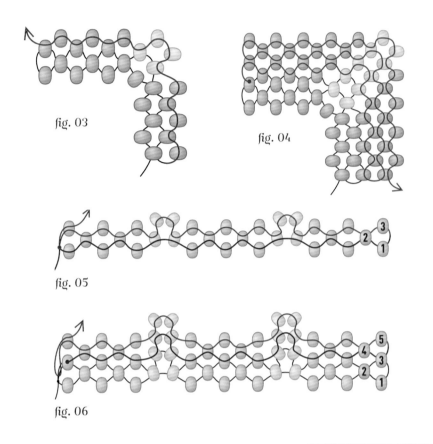

fig. 03

fig. 04

fig. 05

fig. 06

bone pairs in subsequent rows/ rounds. Notice that the work begins to expand as you peyote-stitch more beads before and after the herringbone corners *(fig. 04)*.

### mid-row herringbone columns

Work columns of herringbone between sections of flat peyote stitch for a decorative look. String an odd number of beads for the peyote sections and 2 beads for the herringbone columns; repeat the sequence as desired. Learn the technique by following this sample with 5 beads between each herringbone pair:

**ROWS 1 AND 2** String a sequence of 5 blue beads and 2 gold beads twice. String 5 blue beads *(fig. 05, blue)*.

**ROW 3** String 1 blue bead, skip 1 blue bead previously strung, and pass through the next bead; repeat twice. String 2 gold beads and pass through the next gold bead of Row 1 (this forms the first herringbone stitch). Repeat the entire sequence. String 1 blue bead, skip 1 blue bead previously strung, and pass through the next bead; repeat. String 1 blue bead, tie the tail and working

threads together with a square knot, and pass back through the last blue bead added *(fig. 05, red)*. note: *When counting rows, count the first two columns along one of the peyote sides, not the number of herringbone pairs.*

**ROW 4** Work 2 peyote stitches with 1 blue bead in each stitch. Work 1 herringbone stitch with 2 gold beads and pass through the next blue bead of the previous row. Repeat the entire sequence. Work 2 peyote stitches with 1 blue bead in each stitch *(fig. 06, blue)*.

**ROW 5** Work 3 peyote stitches with 1 blue bead in each stitch. Work 1 herringbone stitch with 2 gold beads. Repeat the entire sequence. Work 2 peyote stitches with 1 blue bead in each stitch. String 1 blue bead, pass the needle around the previous thread loop at the side of the beadwork, and pass back through the last blue bead added to work an odd-count turnaround *(fig. 06, red)*.

**ROWS 6 AND ON** Repeat Rows 4 and 5. note: *If you see a small gap with thread showing between the gold beads of Row 2, consider adding 1 size 15° or size 11° between each pair when stringing Rows 1 and 2. This also helps keep the work straight and flat if yours tends to bend.*

### mid-round herringbone columns

You can also add columns of herringbone between sections of circular peyote stitch. String an odd

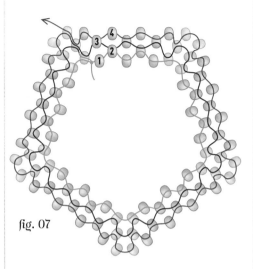

fig. 07

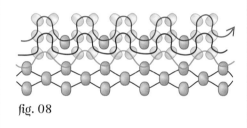

fig. 08

number of beads for the peyote sections and 2 beads for the herringbone columns; repeat the sequence as desired. Learn the technique by following this sample with 5 beads between each herringbone pair:

**ROUNDS 1 AND 2** String a sequence of 2 gold beads and 5 blue beads five times. Tie a square knot to form a circle and exit the first gold bead strung, making sure the knot doesn't slip inside the bead *(fig. 07, green)*.

**ROUND 3** *String 2 gold beads and pass through the next gold bead of the previous round (this forms the first herringbone stitch). String 1 blue bead, skip 1 blue bead previously strung, and pass through the next bead; repeat twice. Repeat from * four times. Step up through the first bead of this round *(fig. 07, blue)*.

**ROUND 4** Work 1 herringbone stitch with 2 gold beads. Work 4 peyote stitches with 1 blue bead in each. Repeat the entire sequence four times. Step up through the first bead of this round *(fig. 07, red)*.

**ROUNDS 5 AND ON** Repeat Round 4, working 1 additional peyote stitch in each peyote section. Control the shape of the beadwork by working increases or changing bead size in the peyote sections—depending on what you desire, you can control the increases to keep the work flat or to make it ruffle.

### peyote-to-herringbone transition

To transition from peyote to herringbone stitch, begin by working a row/round with 2 beads in each stitch *(fig. 08, green)*.

To stitch the second row/round, work herringbone stitch with 2 beads in each stitch *(fig. 08, blue)*.

If the herringbone section is narrower than the peyote section, you can control the shaping by adding 1 or more beads between each herringbone column *(fig. 08, red)*.

### herringbone-to-peyote transition

To work peyote stitch off herringbone stitch, work the final row/round of herringbone with 1 bead in each stitch *(fig. 09, blue)*. Then work peyote stitch off the last row/round of beads, stitching 1 bead between each previous bead *(fig. 09, red)*. Alternatively, you could work the final row/round of herringbone with 3 beads in each stitch and pass through only the center bead at the top of each column when adding the first row/round of peyote.

**101**

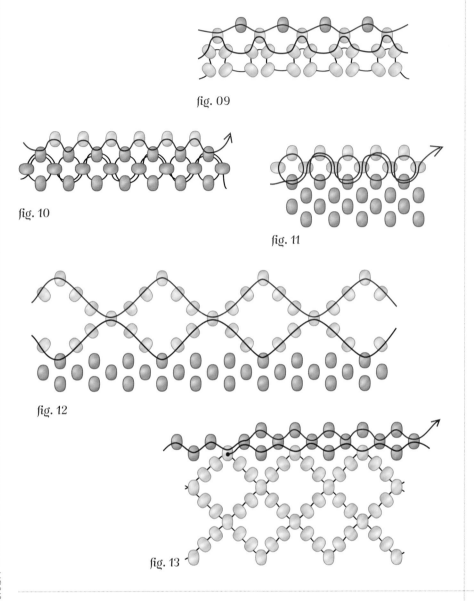

fig. 09

fig. 10

fig. 11

fig. 12

fig. 13

The example shown will cause the beadwork to decrease along the top edge, making it a perfect way to close a herringbone-stitched bezel. If you wish the work to remain flat, use larger beads or more beads in each peyote stitch.

## right-angle-weave combination

Because the top bead of each right-angle-weave unit is horizontal, this stitch is the perfect match for peyote stitch.

### *peyote-to–right-angle-weave transition*

Simply exit the top bead in any unit, string 1 bead, and pass through the top bead of the next right-angle-weave unit; repeat peyote stitching *(fig. 10)*. Whether working with flat or circular right-angle weave, the technique is the same.

### *right-angle-weave-to-peyote transition*

Work right-angle-weave units off peyote up beads *(fig. 11)*. If the right-angle-weave beads are larger than the peyote beads, consider stitching the right-angle-weave units to every other peyote up bead.

## netting combinations

Netting stitches are similar to picots because each stitch consists of 3 or more beads. Picots are usually purely decorative and added as a finishing touch to a project, whereas nets are seen mid-row/round as structural elements. Each net is typically made with an odd number of beads so that the center bead forms a peak; subsequent rows/rounds are worked off this center bead.

### peyote-to-netting transition

Exiting an up bead of a peyote stitch row/round, string the net beads and pass through the next up bead. Or, if working large nets, skip over several peyote beads **(fig. 12, blue)**. Step up through the center bead of the nearest net to prepare for the next row/round. Stitch the next row/round of nets to the center beads of the previous nets **(fig. 12, red)**.

### netting-to-peyote transition

Exit the center of a net in the final row/round, string 3 beads (or any odd number needed to bridge the gap between nets), and pass through the center of the next net; repeat for the length of the work **(fig. 13, blue)**. When setting up for the next row/round, be sure to exit a bead strung just before or just after the center of the net and not the center net bead. Work a row/round of peyote stitch off the beads just added **(fig. 13, red)**.

## DESIGNING BEADWORK

Now that you have the ins and outs of peyote under your belt and the ability to smoothly transition from peyote to herringbone, right-angle weave, and netting, you're ready to venture out into the world of design. Here are few tips to get you started:

● **Start slow.** Don't expect to create an original masterpiece the first time. Instead, pick two or three favorite projects and combine elements of each into a piece that's uniquely you. Or, pick just one project and personalize the colors and add extra embellishment.

● **Use a chart.** It's easy to find free peyote-stitch graph paper online for both flat and circular variations. Print them out, color the beads in a fun pattern you enjoy, and start beading.

● **Expect trial and error.** It's not uncommon for me to have a handful of samples before I land on the correct bead counts and thread paths that complete my vision. Once I figure out the structure, then I create the second handful of samples to test color.

● **Who is your audience?** If you're designing a piece you want to teach or publish, keep in mind the complexity of each move as you bead. Remember, you'll not only need to replicate what you did, but you'll also need to illustrate it and teach it. If you're beading something just

for you or a one-of-a-kind piece, have fun and get as elaborate as you want!

● **Give yourself an assignment.** It's easy to get overwhelmed with the irresistible bead colors and shapes on the market today. Hone in on one color palette and limit your bead shapes and sizes. You'll be amazed by what can result from a focused set of materials.

● **Get feedback.** Don't be afraid to reach out to fellow beaders for their advice and know-how. Meet beaders at your local bead shop and seek them out on Facebook, where there's an amazingly large community of beaders.

● **Break it down.** Overwhelmed by the thought of creating an entire piece start to finish? Start with the elements: bead just a rope for a lampwork pendant, bead a focal for a silver chain, or make some beaded-bead earrings. Soon you'll be ready to put it all together.

● **Mute muse?** If you feel any pressure trying to express your inner voice in your artwork, relax and think of designing for someone else (real or fictitious). Let his or her style and personality be your inspiration.

● **Try it on.** With jewelry, there's sometimes no other way to catch an error like a too-short toggle clasp or a pendant that hangs awkwardly. This also helps you understand the drape of the piece, calculate length, and determine bead placement.

Who says freeform peyote stitch has to be wild? In this project, you'll begin with a petal framework, then work each petal in a freeform way to achieve a look that's both structured and organic. It's a perfect project for those who love a little order with their chaos. Plus, you're free from the task of following a pattern bead by bead.

● *by jean campbell*

# daisy girl

**TECHNIQUES**
Freeform, circular, and flat peyote stitch

Crimping

Stringing

Whipstitch

Zipping

Fringe

**MATERIALS**
1 g light blue matte size 15° Japanese seed beads (A)

4 g lemon chiffon matte size 11° Czech seed beads (B)

4 g lavender blue opaque luster size 11° Japanese seed beads (C)

4 g dark aqua–lined amethyst size 11° Japanese seed beads (D)

4 g purple-lined clear size 11° Japanese seed beads (E)

410 light blue 6mm crystal pearls

3 sterling silver 2mm crimp tubes

Crystal 6 lb braided beading thread

9' (2.7 m) of gray .018 or .019 flexible beading wire

**TOOLS**
Scissors

Size 12 beading needle

2 pairs of chain- or flat-nose pliers

Crimping pliers

Wire cutters

**FINISHED SIZE**
30" (76.2 cm) necklace (shortest strand); 2⅜" (6 cm) flower

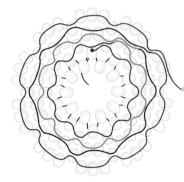

fig. 01: stitching the base

## 1 strands.

**strands.** String pearls to form the necklace strands:

**STRAND 1** Use 3' (.9 m) of beading wire to string 125 pearls and 1 crimp tube. Pass the other end back through the tube to form a circle. Snug the pearls, crimp the tube, and trim the excess wire. Set aside.

**STRAND 2** Repeat Strand 1 using 132 pearls.

**STRAND 3** Repeat Strand 1 using 138 pearls.

## 2 base.

**base.** Work circular peyote stitch to form the center of the flower:

**BASE, ROUNDS 1 AND 2** Use 8' (2.4 m) of thread to string 20B, leaving a 2' (.6 m) tail. Tie a square knot with the tail and working threads to form a circle. Pass through the first bead

strung, making sure the knot doesn't slip inside the bead.

**BASE, ROUND 3** String 1B, skip 1B previously strung, and pass through the next B; repeat to add a total of 10B. Step up through the first B added in this round *(fig. 01, purple)*.

**BASE, ROUND 4** Work 10 stitches with 2B in each stitch to add a total of 20B. Step up through the first 2B added in this round *(fig. 01, green)*.

**BASE, ROUND 5** Work 1B in each stitch to add a total of 10B, treating each 2B of Round 4 as 1 bead. Step up through the first B added in this round *(fig. 01, blue)*.

**BASE, ROUND 6** Work 10 stitches with 3B in each stitch to add a total of 30B *(fig. 01, red)*. No step up is needed; exit from 1B of Round 5.

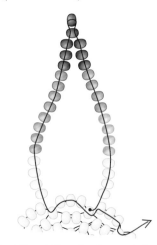

fig. 02: adding the first petal

fig. 03: filling the center of the petal

fig. 04: zipping the center

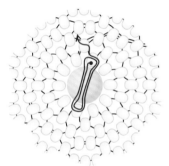

fig. 05: adding the
center pearl

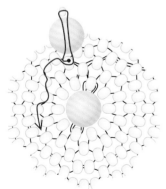

fig. 06: stitching the
first pearl fringe

**3 petals.** Stitch a framework of petals, then work freeform circular peyote stitch within the individual petal loops:

**PETAL LOOPS** String 4B, 4C, 4D, and 5E; pass back through the fourth E. String 3E, 4D, 4C, and 4B; pass through the previous B of Round 5, the next 3B of Round 6, and the B from Round 5 where this petal began. Pass through the next 3B of Round 6 and the following B of Round 5 *(fig. 02)*. Repeat this entire section nine times to add a total of 10 petal loops, layering each so the right side of the new petal overlaps the left side of the previous one. Exit from the first B added to the final petal.

**FILL, ROUND 1** Work 7 circular peyote stitches inside of 1 petal loop with 1 size 11° in each stitch, choosing between B, C, D, and E beads as desired. Skip the tip of the petal, pass down through the sixth E added in the petal loop, and continue working circular peyote stitch down the petal loop and along the B in Base Round 6, adding a total of 17 beads in this round. Exit from the first bead added in this round *(fig. 03)*. note: *Be sure all the beads just added are flipped toward the center of the petal.*

**FILL, ROUNDS 2 AND ON** Continue working in circular peyote stitch, making decreases as necessary to shape the petal. It works well to make decreases at the tip of the petal as in Fill Round 1, but making decreases near the base

will be necessary as well. note: *It's not that important where the decreases are made because the flower's character comes from this randomness. What is important is that the center of the petal is generally filled to your liking. Work enough rounds to cause the petals to curl.*

**ZIP** When the beads of the inner round of the petal touch, interlock the beads and zip them together to close the petal *(fig. 04)*. Weave through beads to exit from the first B of the next petal loop.

Repeat the fill for each petal loop, making each petal a little different from the next. As you work, embrace color variation from petal to petal by placing the B, C, D, and E in slightly different spots than you did in the previous petal. You can also try changing the bead counts and decrease spots from petal to petal, making some petals thinner, some wider. This all adds to the natural quality of your final piece. Secure the working thread and trim; don't trim the tail.

**4 flower center.** Add pearls to the flower center:

**CENTER** Use the tail thread to string 1 pearl; pass through a B on the opposite side of Base Round 1. Pass back through the pearl and the original B exited. Repeat the thread path to reinforce and exit from the nearest B in Base Round 2 *(fig. 05)*.

**FRINGE** String 1 pearl and 1A; pass back through the pearl and the

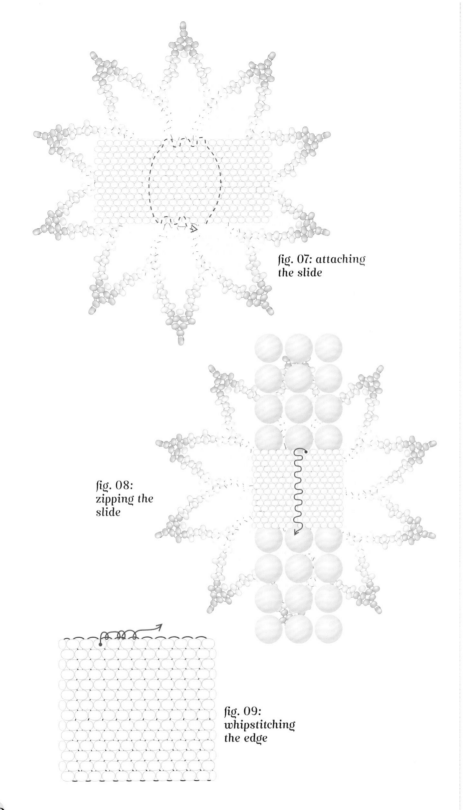

fig. 07: attaching
the slide

fig. 08:
zipping the
slide

fig. 09:
whipstitching
the edge

back of slide

last B exited on the base to form
a fringe. Weave through beads
to exit 1½ pearl widths from the
last pearl placed *(fig. 06)*. Repeat
thirteen times to add a total of
14 fringes placed in a pleasing
arrangement at the center of the
flower. Secure the thread and
trim. Set the flower aside.

**5** **slide.** Use flat peyote stitch
to make a slide that connects
the flower to the pearl strands:

**STRIP** Use 4' (1.2 m) of thread to
peyote-stitch a strip 14B wide
and 44 rows long, leaving an
8" (20.3 cm) tail. Weave the
working thread through beads to
exit from an edge bead near the
middle of the strip.

**CONNECT** Center the strip on the
back of the flower. Securely stitch
the strip to the base of each petal
on the back of the flower, tacking
petals down as you go *(fig. 07)*.

**ZIP** Lay the crimped sections of the pearl strands on the back of the strip, behind the flower. Be sure the strands are in size order (with Strand 2 in the middle). Fold the strip so the first and last rows touch. Use the tail thread to zip the beads together to form a seamless tube around the pearl strands *(fig. 08)*.

**REINFORCE** Use the extra tail and working threads to whipstitch the threads at the edges of the strip to reinforce *(fig. 09)*. Secure the thread and trim.

## TIPS

● The irregularity of Czech seed beads is an advantage in this project. Choose slightly skinny or slightly large beads as needed when filling the petal centers.

● While working the petal centers, keep in mind that you're working freeform peyote stitch: It's not going to look symmetrical or smooth . . . on purpose! Think of the irregularities in nature, and you'll find that this type of beading is a great way to mimic the imperfection in real flowers.

● If your first petal isn't quite what you thought it would be, go ahead and stitch the second one. You may be surprised to find how nice the second petal makes the first one look.

● Avoid adding too many beads at the base and tip of each petal when filling. This will give you two straight, easy-to-zip edges down the center.

## DESIGN OPTION

● To achieve the look of a 5-petal flower with 5 leaves, start by alternating pink and green for the loops in Step 3. When filling the petals, manipulate the loops so the pink petals sit on top of the green leaves. Before zipping the leaves, be sure they curl down; when zipping the petals, be sure they curl up. Turn the flower into a brooch by adding a pin back behind the base.

Dozens of three-dimensional beaded beads decorate a silver neck wire in this boldly textured necklace. Jean's desire to make a triangle-shaped beaded bead from one beadwoven piece, instead of piecing several parts together, inspired her to devise this unique pattern. Her soft, muted color choices were inspired by a misty urban skyline. • *by jean power*

# urban skyline

### TECHNIQUES
Tubular and flat peyote stitch

Herringbone stitch

Zipping

Stringing

### MATERIALS
1 g silver matte metallic size 11° cylinder beads

2 g each of size 11° cylinder beads in ice blue Ceylon, gray matte, and lilac Ceylon

3 g each of size 11° cylinder beads in sea blue Ceylon, ice blue matte, sea blue matte, heather matte metallic, silver-lined gray, and heather metallic iris

4 g each of size 11° cylinder beads in purple silver metallic and light gray luster

5 g silver-lined blue-gray size 11° cylinder beads

14 g gray matte metallic size 11° cylinder beads

1 silver 6¼" (15.9 cm) diameter neck wire with screw-on 6mm ball ends

Size D nylon thread in colors to match beads

### TOOLS
Scissors

Size 12 beading needles

### FINISHED SIZE
18" (45.7 cm)

### TIPS
● Purchase a matching silver bangle and wear just a few of the collar's beaded beads at a time, mixing and matching colors as desired.

● For bigger beaded beads, simply substitute size 10° cylinder beads; for smaller beaded beads, use size 15° cylinder beads. You may need to add or remove rounds depending on the look you're after, but the principle and basic steps remain the same.

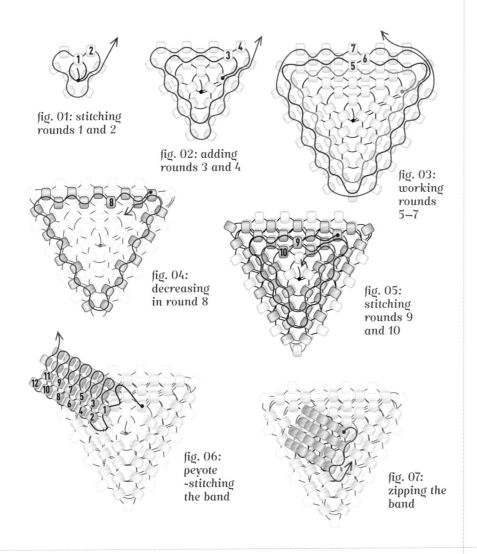

fig. 01: stitching rounds 1 and 2

fig. 02: adding rounds 3 and 4

fig. 03: working rounds 5–7

fig. 04: decreasing in round 8

fig. 05: stitching rounds 9 and 10

fig. 06: peyote-stitching the band

fig. 07: zipping the band

*herringbone stitch.* String 1 bead; pass through next bead of Round 2 to work a peyote stitch. Repeat the entire sequence twice to add a total of 9 beads *(fig. 02, blue)*.

**ROUND 4** String 2 beads; pass through the next bead of Round 3. Work 2 peyote stitches with 1 bead in each stitch. Repeat the entire sequence twice to add a total of 12 beads *(fig. 02, red)*.

**ROUND 5** String 2 beads; pass through the next bead of Round 4. Work 3 peyote stitches with 1 bead in each stitch. Repeat the entire sequence twice to add a total of 15 beads *(fig. 03, green)*.

**ROUND 6** String 1 bead and pass through the next bead of Round 5; repeat fourteen times to add a total of 15 beads *(fig. 03, blue)*.

**ROUND 7** Repeat Round 6 *(fig. 03, red)*. note: *Round 7 forms the outermost edge of the beaded bead. The rounds will decrease from this point on to form the back of the beaded bead.*

## 2 beaded triangle back.

Work decreasing peyote stitches to form the back of the beaded bead with silver matte metallic size 11° cylinder beads:

**ROUND 8** Work 4 peyote stitches with 1 bead in each stitch and, without adding a bead, pass through the next bead of Round 7 to form a decrease; repeat twice. Step up for each new round by passing through the first bead added in the current round *(fig. 04)*.

**ROUND 9** Work 3 peyote stitches with 1 bead in each stitch and,

## 1 beaded triangle front.

Use a combination of tubular peyote and herringbone stitches to form the front of the beaded bead with silver matte metallic size 11° cylinder beads:

**ROUND 1** Use 2' (.6 m) of thread to string 3 beads, leaving an 8" (20.3 cm) tail. Tie a square knot with the tail and working threads to form a circle. Pass through the first bead strung, making sure

the knot doesn't slip inside the bead *(fig. 01, blue)*.

**ROUND 2** String 2 beads and pass through the next bead of Round 1; repeat twice to add a total of 6 beads. Step up for each new round by passing through the first bead added in the current round *(fig. 01, red)*.

**ROUND 3** String 2 beads; pass through the next bead of Round 2. note: *This forms the first*

without adding a bead, pass through the next bead of Round 8 to form a decrease; repeat twice *(fig. 05, blue)*.

**ROUND 10** Work 2 peyote stitches with 1 bead in each stitch and, without adding a bead, pass through the next bead of Round 9 to form a decrease; repeat twice *(fig. 05, red)*.

**3 band.** Use flat peyote stitch to create a band on the back of the beaded bead with silver matte metallic size 11° cylinder beads:

**ROW 1** String 1 bead and pass through next bead of Round 10; repeat *(fig. 06, blue)*.

**ROWS 2–12** Working off Row 1 with 1 bead in each stitch, use flat peyote stitch to make a strip 4 beads wide and 12 rows long *(fig. 06, red)*.

**ZIP** Fold the strip over to meet the opposite side of Round 10. Zip the beads of Row 12 to the beads of Round 10 to close the band *(fig. 07)*. Secure the threads and trim.

Repeat Steps 1–3 seventy times to create a total of 71 beaded beads using the following colors: Make 1 ice blue Ceylon, 2 gray matte, 2 lilac Ceylon, 3 sea blue Ceylon, 4 ice blue matte, 4 heather matte metallic, 4 sea blue matte, 5 silver-lined gray, 5 heather metallic iris, 6 purple silver metallic, 6 light gray luster, 8 silver-lined blue-gray, and 20 gray matte metallic.

**4 finishing.** Unscrew the ball at one end of the neck wire. String the beaded beads onto the neck wire, varying the colors to create a random pattern. If you want the beaded beads to point in the same direction as the sample, pass through the side of the band that lines up with a triangle point. Or, for a random look, don't pay attention to the direction of the triangle points as you string. Screw the ball back on the end of the neck wire.

## TIPS

● To give the beaded components a completely different feel, work them using size 11° Japanese seed beads. The rounded nature of these beads will give the beadwork a softer look.

● You can use the same basic steps to make a coordinating ring. Make the triangle as large as you desire and the band long enough to fit around your finger, and you'll have a piece to match your necklace in no time.

## DESIGN OPTIONS

Try these fun-and-simple variations when creating your own unique set of beaded beads:

● In this mostly mauve bead, Jean has a little bit of fun with color, using bronze for Rounds 4 and 5.

● For a larger beaded bead (like Jean's red-and-matte-white variation), repeat Round 5 twice more, adding an extra bead on each side. (On the first extra round, you'll have 4 peyote stitches on each side between the herringbone beads; on the second round, you'll have 5.) Then continue beading using the same principle as the basic beads and working 2 extra rounds when decreasing on the back side. You can change color at any time.

● Add some dimension to the beaded bead by stitching a little tower at the top. Start with Rounds 1 and 2 as usual, then work 6 rounds of tubular peyote stitch with 1 bead in each stitch. (You'll need to split the herringbone pairs of Round 2 so the first round of tubular peyote stitch consists of 6 beads.) The tower can be tall (like the gold tower on the purple bead) or it can be short (like the navy tower on the gray matte bead), just be sure to work an even number of rounds so the corners line up. Close the top by passing through the center bead of each side. Weave down through the tower to exit Round 2 and resume beading the bead as usual.

A square, a triangle, and a circle adorn the ends of a crystal-studded bead chain in this reversible lariat-style necklace. Create the three-dimensional shapes using peyote and netting. Geometry has never been more fun! ● *by cynthia rutledge*

# pi r-squared lariat

**TECHNIQUES**
Flat and tubular peyote stitch

Netting

Picot

Zipping

**MATERIALS**
1 g medium lavender–lined light mauve size 15° seed beads (A)

1 g transparent celery luster size 15° seed beads (B)

1 g gilt-lined aqua size 15° seed beads (C)

1 g gold-lined crystal AB size 15° seed beads (D)

1 g green metallic AB size 15° seed beads (E)

1 g transparent pale green size 15° seed beads (F)

2 g antique silver metallic size 15° seed beads (G)

3 g higher-metallic lavender AB size 11° cylinder beads (H)

2 g turquoise-lined light turquoise AB size 11° cylinder beads (I)

3 g higher-metallic white gold AB size 11° cylinder beads (J)

3 g higher-metallic green gold AB size 11° cylinder beads (K)

3 g green/bronze metallic AB size 11° cylinder beads (L)

2 g raspberry-lined metallic raspberry size 11° cylinder beads (M)

12 chrysolite 2XAB 3mm crystal bicones (N)

12 indicolite 2XAB 3mm crystal bicones (O)

10 azore 3mm crystal bicones (P)

10 jonquil satin 3mm crystal bicones (Q)

12 light rose satin 3mm crystal bicones (R)

12 erinite 3mm crystal bicones (S)

12 aquamarine satin 3mm crystal bicones (T)

12 Pacific opal 3mm crystal bicones (U)

10 olivine 2XAB 3mm crystal bicones (V)

22 cantaloupe 3mm crystal bicones (W)

12 aquamarine champagne 3mm crystal bicones (X)

24" (.6 m) of silver-plated beaded chain with 3.5×4mm oval links and aquamarine purple haze 6mm crystal rounds

4 sterling silver 4mm 22-gauge jump rings

Nylon beading thread in light beige, gray, and green

Microcrystalline wax

**TOOLS**
Size 12 beading needles

Scissors

2 pairs of chain- or flat-nose pliers

**FINISHED SIZE**
33" (.8 m)

**1 triangle.** Start with a strip of flat peyote stitch, join the ends into a ring, and then work tubular peyote and netting stitches to form a reversible triangle embellished with crystals and picots:

**ROWS 1 AND 2** Use 6' (1.8 m) of waxed gray thread to string 48H, leaving a 6" (15.2 cm) tail *(fig. 01, blue)*.

**ROW 3** String 1H, skip the 1H previously strung, and pass through the next H; repeat twenty-three times to add a total of 24H *(fig. 01, red)*.

**JOIN** Add a needle to the tail thread and pass through the last bead of Row 1, the nearest bead of Row 2, and the next bead of Row 1 *(fig. 02, blue)*. Pass the working thread through the first bead of Row 3, the nearest bead of Row 2, and the next bead of Row 3 *(fig. 02, red)*. Pull both threads to tighten the strip into a ring. *note: You will now begin working in rounds.*

**ROUND 4** String 2A; pass through the next H of Round 3. Work 7 tubular peyote stitches with 1H in each stitch. Repeat the entire sequence twice to add a total of 6A and 21H. Step up through the first A added in this round *(fig. 03, blue)*.

**ROUND 5** Work tubular peyote stitch with 1H in each stitch to add a total of 27H, splitting the pairs of A at each corner. Step up through the first H added in this round *(fig. 03, red)*.

**ROUND 6** String 1H and pass through the next H of Round 5, nearest H of Round 4, and next H

of Round 5 to form a decrease; repeat three times. String 1H; pass through the next 1H of Round 5. Repeat the entire sequence twice to add a total of 15H. Step up through the first H added in this round *(fig. 04, blue)*.

**ROUND 7** String 1A, 1N, and 1A and pass through the next H of Round 6; repeat three times. String 3H; pass through the next H of Round 6. Repeat the entire sequence twice to add a total of 24A, 12N, and 9H. Step up through the first A/N/A net added in this round *(fig. 04, red)*.

**ROUND 8** String 1H and pass through the next A/N/A net of Round 7; repeat twice. String 1H; pass through the next 3H of Round 7. String 1H; pass through the next A/N/A net of Round 7. Repeat the entire sequence twice to add a total of 15H. Step up through the first H added in this round *(fig. 05, green)*.

**ROUND 9** String 1A and pass through the next N of Round 7, then string 1A and pass through the next H of Round 8; repeat twice. String 1H; skip 1H of Round 7, and pass through the

next H of Round 7. String 1H; pass through the next H of Round 8. String 1A; pass through the next N of Round 7. String 1A; pass through the next H of Round 8. Repeat the entire sequence twice to add a total of 24A and 6H. Step up through the first A added in this round *(fig. 05, blue)*.

**ROUND 10** String 3B; pass through the next A of Round 9 to form a picot. String 1H; pass through the next A of Round 9. Repeat the entire sequence fourteen times to add a total of fifteen 3B picots and 15H, forming a picot over each crystal and at each corner. Secure the tail thread and trim. Weave the working thread through beads to exit 1H of Row 1, just before a corner *(fig. 05, red)*.

**ROUND 11** Working off Row 1 beads and making sure the corners align, repeat Round 4.

**ROUNDS 12–16** Repeat Rounds 5–9 using O in place of N in Round 14.

**ROUND 17 AND ZIP** String 3B and pass through the next bead (the nearest A or H) of Round 16, the next H of Round 10, and the next bead (the nearest A or H) of Round 16 *(fig. 06)*. Repeat the entire sequence fourteen times to zip the sides together and to add a total of fifteen 3B picots.

**TOP LOOP** Weave through beads to exit 1H of Round 10 before a corner. String 9A, skip the 3B of Round 10, and pass through the next H of Round 10 *(fig. 07)*. Weave through beads to reinforce the thread path.

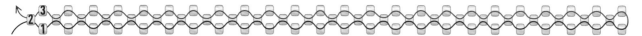

fig. 01: working rows 1–3 of the triangle

fig. 02: joining the ends of the starting rows to form a ring

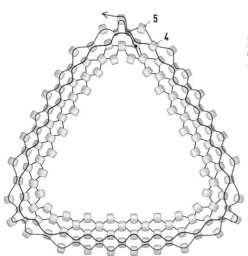

fig. 03: stitching rounds 4 and 5 of the triangle

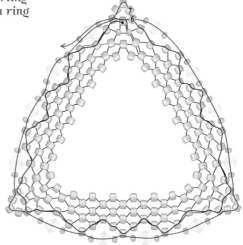

fig. 04: adding rounds 6 and 7 of the triangle

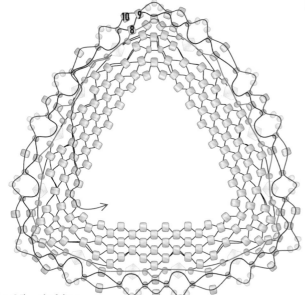

fig. 05: stitching rounds 8–10 of the triangle

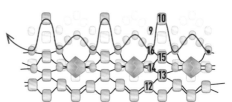

fig. 06: adding round 17 picots and zipping the 2 sides of the triangle

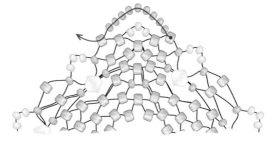

fig. 07: adding the top loop to the triangle

**BOTTOM LOOP** Weave through beads to the side of the triangle that's opposite the loop just made. Exit the center B of a Round 10 picot that's second from a corner. String 9A; pass through the center B of the next Round 10 picot. Pass through the center B of the nearest Round 17 picot, exiting toward the start of the loop *(fig. 08, blue)*. String 1A; skip 1A and pass back through the next 7A of the loop. String 1A; pass through the center bead of the next Round 17 picot. Work a turnaround to exit the center B of the nearest Round 10 picot. Repeat the thread path to reinforce. Secure the thread and trim *(fig. 08, red)*.

Repeat this entire step to form a second triangle, using J in place H, G in place of A, C in place of B, W in place of N, and X in place of O. Omit the bottom loop. Set the triangles aside.

**2 circle.** Start with a strip of flat peyote stitch, join the ends into a ring, and then work tubular peyote and netting stitches to form a reversible circle embellished with crystals:

**ROWS 1 AND 2** Use 5' (1.5 m) of waxed gray thread to string 40I, leaving a 6" (15.2 cm) tail.

**ROW 3** Repeat Step 1, Row 3 using 1I in each stitch to add a total of 20I.

**JOIN** Join the ends of the strip as in Step 1 to form a ring. **note:** *You will now begin working in rounds.*

**ROUNDS 4–7** Work tubular peyote with 1I in each stitch to add a

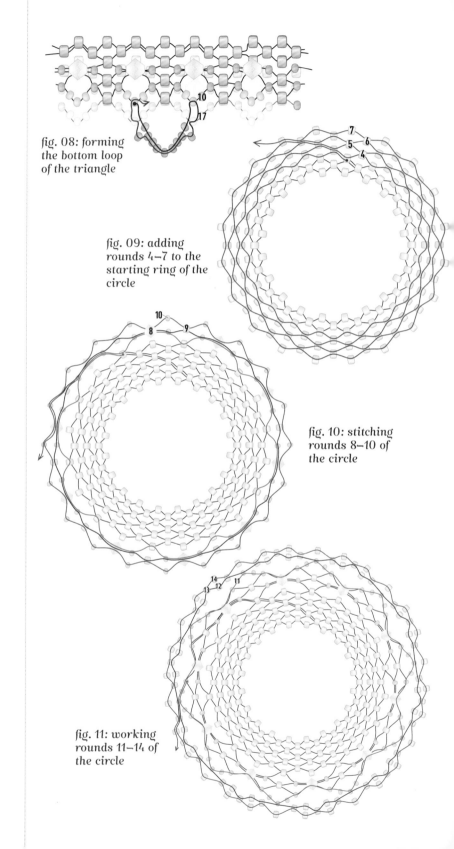

fig. 08: forming the bottom loop of the triangle

fig. 09: adding rounds 4–7 to the starting ring of the circle

fig. 10: stitching rounds 8–10 of the circle

fig. 11: working rounds 11–14 of the circle

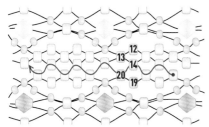

fig. 12: zipping outside of the circle

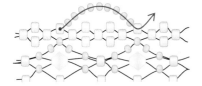

fig. 13: adding the first loop to the circle

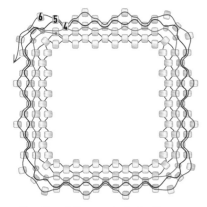

fig. 14: adding rounds 4–6 to the starting ring of the square

total of 20I in each of 4 rounds. Step up through the first I added in each round *(fig. 09, red)*.

**ROUND 8** String 1C, 1P, and 1C, then skip the next I of Round 7 and pass through the next I; repeat nine times to add a total of 20C and 10P. Step up through the first C/P/C net added in this round *(fig. 10, green)*.

**ROUND 9** String 1I and pass through the next C/P/C net of Round 8; repeat nine times to add a total of 10I. Step up through the first I added in this round *(fig. 10, blue)*.

**ROUND 10** String 1C and pass through the nearest P of Round 8, then string 1C and pass through the nearest I of Round 9; repeat nine times to add a total of 20C. Step up through the *second* C added in this round *(fig. 10, red)*.

**ROUND 11** String 3C and pass through the next C of Round 10, nearest P of Round 8, and next C of Round 10 to form a net; repeat nine times to add a total of ten 3C nets. Step up through the first 2C added in this round *(fig. 11, green)*.

**ROUNDS 12 AND 13** String 5J and pass through the C at the tip of the next Round 11 net; repeat nine times to add a total of ten 5J nets. Step up through the first J added in this round *(fig. 11, blue)*. note: *Although we're just going around the circle once here, we're adding beads for both Rounds 12 and 13.*

**ROUND 14** Work tubular peyote with 1J in each stitch to add a total of 30J *(fig. 11, red)*. Secure the tail thread and trim. note: *This round will cause the beadwork to roll a bit; make sure that it rolls inward.*

**ROUND 15** Weave through beads to exit a bead of Row 1. Working off Row 1 beads, repeat Round 8 using Q in place of P and making sure the first net aligns with a net added in Round 8. If it doesn't align, pass through 2 more beads to exit the next bead of Row 1 and then begin stitching the round.

**ROUNDS 16–20** Repeat Rounds 9–13.

**ZIP** Pass through 1J of Round 14 and 1J of Round 20; repeat around to zip the sides together *(fig. 12)*.

**LOOPS** Exiting 1J of Round 14, string 9C, skip 2J of Round 14, and pass through the next J *(fig. 13)*. Weave through beads to reinforce the thread path. Weave through beads to exit from Round 14 on the other side of the circle, 12C from the last C exited. Add a second 9C loop in the same manner. Secure the thread and trim. Repeat this entire step to form a second circle using M in place of I, D in place of C, K in place of J, V in place of P, and W in place of Q.

**3 square.** Start with a strip of flat peyote stitch, join the ends into a ring, and then work tubular peyote and netting stitches to form a reversible square embellished with crystals and picots:

**ROWS 1 AND 2** Use 6' (1.8 m) of waxed light beige thread to string 48K, leaving a 6" (15.2 cm) tail.

**ROW 3** Repeat Step 1, Row 3 using 1K in each stitch to add a total of 24K.

**JOIN** Join the ends of the strip as in Step 1 to form a ring. note: *You will now begin working in rounds.*

**ROUND 4** String 2D; pass through the next K of Row 3. Work 5 tubular peyote stitches with 1K in each stitch. Repeat the entire sequence three times to add a total of 8D and 20K. Step up through the first D added in this round *(fig. 14, green)*.

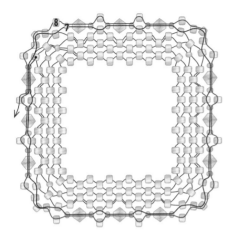

fig. 15: adding rounds 7 and 8 to the square

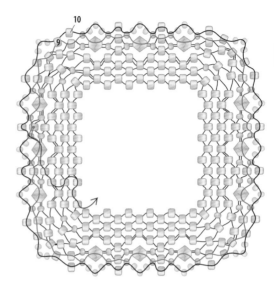

fig. 16: stitching rounds 9 and 10 of the square

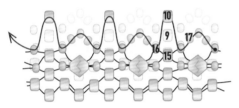

fig. 17: adding round 17 picots and zipping the two sides of the square

fig. 18: adding a loop to a corner of the square

fig. 19: attaching the loop of a square to the chain with jump rings

**ROUND 5** Work tubular peyote with 1K in each stitch to add a total of 28K, splitting the pairs of D at each corner. Step up through the first K added in this round *(fig. 14, blue)*.

**ROUND 6** String 1K and pass through the next K of Round 5, nearest K of Round 4, and next K of Round 5 to form a decrease; repeat twice. String 1K; pass through the next K of Round 5. Repeat the entire sequence three times to add a total of 16K. Step up through the first K added in this round *(fig. 14, red)*.

**ROUND 7** String 1D, 1R, and 1D, then pass through the next K of Round 6; repeat twice. String 3K; pass through the next K of Round 6. Repeat the entire sequence three times to add a total of 12R, 24D, and 12K. Step up through the first D/R/D net added in this round *(fig. 15, blue)*.

**ROUND 8** Work tubular peyote stitch with 1K in each stitch, treating the D/R/D nets and 3K nets of Round 7 as 1 bead, to add a total of 16K. Step up through first K added in this round *(fig. 15, red)*.

**ROUND 9** String 1D and pass through the next R of Round 7, then string 1D and pass through the next K of Round 8; repeat. *String 1K, skip 1K of Round 7, and pass through the next K of Round 7. String 1K; pass through the next K of Round 8. String 1D and pass through the next R of Round 7, then string 1D and pass through the next K of Round 8; repeat twice. Repeat from * twice. String 1K, skip 1K of Round 7, and pass through the next K of Round 7. String 1K; pass through the next K of Round 8. String 1D; pass through the next R of Round 7. String 1D; pass through the next K of Round 8 to add a grand total of 24D and 8K. Step up through the first D added this round *(fig. 16, green)*.

**ROUND 10** String 3B; pass through the next bead of Round 9 to form a picot. String 1K; pass through the next bead of Round 9. Repeat the entire sequence fifteen times to add a total of sixteen 3B picots and 16K, forming a picot over each crystal and at each corner *(fig. 16, blue)*. Secure the tail thread and trim. Weave the working thread through beads to exit 1K of Row 1, just before a corner *(fig. 16, red)*.

**ROUND 11** Working off the beads of Row 1 and making sure the corners align, repeat Round 4.

**ROUNDS 12–16** Repeat Rounds 5–9 using S in place of R in Round 14.

**ROUND 17 AND ZIP** String 3B; pass through the next bead (the nearest D or K) of Round 16,

the next K of Round 10, and the next bead (the nearest D or K) of Round 16 *(fig. 17)*. Repeat the entire sequence fifteen times to zip the sides together and to add a total of sixteen 3B picots.

**LOOP** Weave through beads to exit 1K of Round 10 before a corner. String 11D; pass through the next 1K of Round 10 *(fig. 18)*. Weave through beads to reinforce the thread path. Secure the thread and trim.

Repeat this entire step to form a second square using green thread and L in place of K, E in place of D, F in place of B, U in place of R, and T in place of S. Add a second loop on the opposite corner from the first one.

**4 assembly.** Join the shapes with small beaded rings, then connect the chain using jump rings:

**BEADED RING** Use 1' (.3 m) of waxed gray thread to string 13G, leaving a 6" (15.2 cm) tail. Pass through the top loop of the white gold triangle and 1 of the loops on the pink-and-gold circle. Tie the threads together with a square knot to form a beaded ring. Secure the threads and trim. Join the other loop of the circle to 1 loop of the green square in the same manner.

**JUMP RINGS** Use 2 jump rings to attach the other end of the green square to one end of the chain *(fig. 19)*.

Repeat this entire step using beaded rings to connect the light gold square to the Pacific opal circle and the other side of the Pacific opal

circle to the loop on the side (not the corner) of the purple triangle. Use the remaining jump rings to connect the tip of the purple triangle to the other end of the chain.

## TIPS

● To control the first set of beads strung when starting a project, wrap the tail around the middle finger of your nondominant hand and wrap the thread with the beads around the outside of your index finger. Then hold the thread and last few beads strung between your thumb and middle finger. Point your index finger to pull the thread away from your thumb, creating a straight line of beads. Use your dominant hand to move the needle parallel to the string of beads as you stitch.

● When stitching with crystals, always tighten your thread by pulling gently and straight ahead. If you pull the thread away from the crystal, you can accidently cut the thread.

● To make your own bead-studded chain, form a simple loop at one end of 3" (7.6 cm) of 20- or 22-gauge wire. String 1 bead and form another simple loop. Join the beaded links with small (4 to 6mm) jump rings. Continue forming links for the desired length of the chain. For quicker links, use eye pins instead of wire so you only need to form 1 loop on each.

Use wine-colored seed beads to create sweet bead caps for rich chocolate-colored pearls. Made with a clever combination of stitches, each cap has columns of herringbone stitch separated by sections of peyote stitch. But don't stop beading after you finish this necklace—use the same beaded components in any design you dream up. ● *by melinda barta*

# beaujolais

## TECHNIQUES
Tubular peyote stitch

Herringbone stitch

Stringing

Crimping

Wirework

## MATERIALS
3 g topaz gold luster iris size 15° Japanese seed beads (A)

3 g cabernet metallic iris size 15° Japanese seed beads (B)

1 g burgundy gold luster size 15° Japanese seed beads (C)

1 g gold bronze metallic iris size 15° Japanese seed beads (D)

1 g bronze-lined jonquil AB size 15° Japanese seed beads (E)

1 g silver-lined topaz AB size 15° Japanese seed beads (F)

111 chocolate peacock 7–7.5mm potato pearls

1 antique brass 10×14mm 2-strand magnetic tube bar clasp

21 brass 2½" (6.4 cm) ball-end head pins with 2mm ball

19 natural brass 9.5mm etched jump rings

8 brass 2mm crimp tubes

7½" (19.1 cm) of natural brass 10mm unsoldered round chain (18 links total)

Smoke 6 lb braided beading thread

38" (96.5 cm) of satin gold .018 19-strand flexible beading wire

## TOOLS
Scissors or thread burner

Size 12 beading needles

Wire cutters

2 pairs of chain- or flat-nose pliers

Round-nose pliers

2 bead stops

Crimping pliers

## FINISHED SIZE
22¾" (57.8 cm)

**1 bead cap body.** Use a combination of herringbone and tubular peyote stitches to make the body of the bead cap:

**ROUNDS 1 AND 2** Use 2' (.6 m) of thread to string {1A, 2B, and 2A} four times for a total of 12A and 8B, leaving an 8" (20.3 cm) tail. Pass through the first 2 beads strung *(fig. 01, blue)*.

**ROUND 3** String 2B; pass through the next B of the starting circle (this forms the first herringbone stitch). String 1A, skip 1A previously strung, and pass through the next bead; repeat (this forms the first 2 peyote stitches). Repeat the entire sequence three times to add a total of 8B and 8A. note: *Step up for each new round by passing through the first bead added in the current round (fig. 01, red).* Use relaxed tension when working this and the subsequent rounds.

**ROUND 4** String 2B; pass through the next B of the previous round and the nearest A. String 1A; pass through the next A and B of the previous round. Repeat the entire sequence three times to add a total of 8B and 4A *(fig. 02)*.

**ROUND 5** String 2B; pass through the next B of the previous round. String 1A and pass through the next bead of the previous round; repeat. Repeat the entire sequence three times to add a total of 8B and 8A *(fig. 03, green)*. note: *The beadwork will naturally begin to cup as you work this round. Encourage the beadwork to take shape by using slightly*

*tighter tension, but don't force the beadwork by tugging hard after each stitch. Otherwise, you could break beads. The subsequent rounds will help the beadwork take on the cupped shape, so there's no need to force it here.*

**ROUND 6** Repeat Round 4 *(fig. 03, blue)*.

**ROUND 7** String 1B; pass through the next B of the previous round. String 1A and pass through the next bead of the previous round; repeat. Repeat the entire sequence three times to add a total of 4B and 8A *(fig. 03, red)*. Secure the thread and trim; don't trim the tail.

**2 bead cap top.** Working off Round 1, use the tail thread to close the top of the cap:

**ROUND 8** Add a needle to the tail thread. String 1A; pass through the next A of Round 1. String 1B; pass through the next A of Round 1. Repeat the entire sequence three times to add a total of 4A and 4B *(fig. 04, green)*.

**ROUND 9** String 1B and pass through the next A of Round 8; repeat three times to add a total of 4B *(fig. 04, blue)*.

**ROUND 10** Pass through the 4B added in Round 9 to close the top of the cap *(fig. 04, red)*. Secure the thread and trim. Repeat Steps 1 and 2 nine times for a total of 10 topaz gold/cabernet bead caps. Repeat

fig. 01: working rounds 1–3

fig. 02: adding round 4

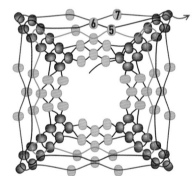

fig. 03: stitching rounds 5–7

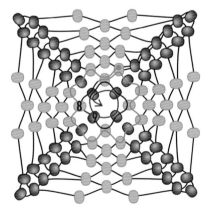

fig. 04: working rounds 8–10 at the top of the cap

fig. 05: finishing
the dangle with a
wrapped loop

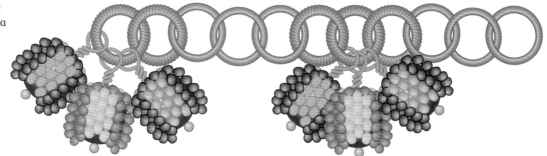

fig. 6: Joining the dangles,
jump rings, and chain segments

Steps 1 and 2 five times using F in place of A for a total of 5 topaz AB/cabernet bead caps. Repeat Steps 1 and 2 five times using E in place of A and D in place of B for a total of 5 jonquil/gold bronze bead caps. Repeat Steps 1 and 2 five times using C in place of B for a total of 5 topaz gold/burgundy bead caps.

Set 4 of the topaz gold/cabernet bead caps aside to string near the clasp in Step 4.

**3 center chain.** Use basic wirework and stringing skills to create pearl clusters with dangles and join them with jump rings and chain segments to form the front of the necklace:

**PEARL CLUSTERS** Use 1 head pin to string 1 pearl and 1 bead cap

(wide end first). Push the bead cap down over the pearl, holding the wire of the head pin with chain-nose pliers, if needed. The bead cap will be snug and "pop" into place. Don't force the bead cap down over the pearl; freshwater pearls vary somewhat

in size so use a slightly smaller pearl instead. Form a wrapped loop **(fig. 05)**. Repeat the entire section twenty times for a total of 21 dangles. Use 1 jump ring to string 3 dangles (choosing the colors at random) and close the jump ring; repeat six times for a total of 7 pearl clusters.

**CHAIN SEGMENTS** Separate the chain into six 3-link segments, opening and closing the chain links as you would jump rings. **note:** *If you substituted the chain used here for chain with soldered links, you'll need to cut the links apart.*

**ASSEMBLY** Use 1 jump ring to join 1 pearl cluster to one end of 1 chain segment. *Use 1 jump ring to attach 1 pearl cluster to

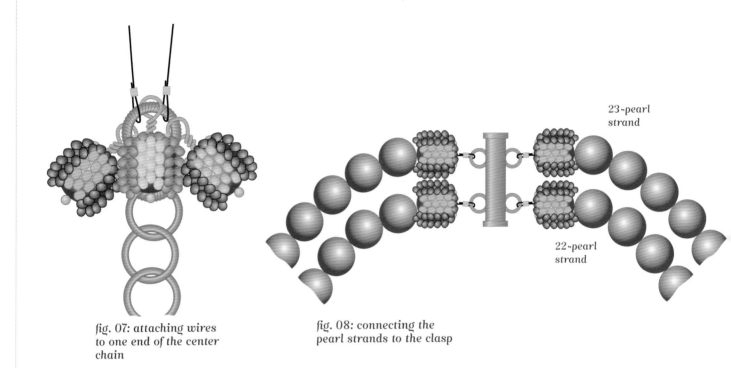

fig. 07: attaching wires
to one end of the center
chain

fig. 08: connecting the
pearl strands to the clasp

23-pearl
strand

22-pearl
strand

the other end of the previous
chain segment. Use 1 jump ring
to attach the same pearl cluster
to one end of another chain
segment, positioning the jump
ring so all the dangles are on
one side of the cluster's ring *(fig.
06)*. note: *Make sure the chain
segments haven't twisted and that
all dangles hang from the same
side of the chain/jump ring strand.*
Repeat from * four times. Use the
remaining jump ring to attach
the last pearl cluster to the free
end of the final chain segment.

**4 finishing.** Create strands
of pearls that connect the
clasp and center chain:

**STRINGING** Use 9½" (24.1 cm) of
beading wire to string 1 crimp
tube and the pearl cluster at one
end of the center chain, passing
the wire around the jump ring
between 2 dangles; pass back
through the tube, crimp, and
trim the excess wire. Repeat to
attach a second wire to the same
pearl cluster, passing around the
jump ring on the other side of
the middle dangle *(fig. 07)*. Use
1 wire to string 23 pearls and 1
wire to string 22 pearls. Clip the
ends of both wires in 1 bead stop
to temporarily hold the pearls in
place.
Repeat this entire step on the
other end of the chain.

**PEARL COUNT CHECK** Hold up the
necklace and, if needed, untwist
the center chain so that all the
dangles hang forward. Check that
the pearls are strung correctly:
the inner strands should have
22 pearls on each and the outer
strands should have 23 pearls on
each to account for the curve of
the necklace. If needed, adjust
the number on each strand.

**CLASP ATTACHMENT** Remove
1 inner 22-pearl strand from the
bead stop and string 1 of the
previously set aside topaz gold
/cabernet bead caps (wide end
first). Push the cap down over
the last pearl. String 1 crimp tube
and the bottom loop of one half

mastering peyote stitch

of the clasp; pass back through the crimp tube, snug the beads, crimp, and trim the excess wire. Remove the bead stop from the outer 23-pearl strand on the same side of the necklace, add a bead cap, and attach it to the top loop of the clasp half just used in the same manner. Remove the remaining bead stop, add bead caps, and attach the 2 strands to the other half of the clasp as before, making sure the clasp aligns correctly when closed *(fig. 08)*.

## TIPS

● When counting rounds, count along one of the peyote-stitch columns, not the number of herringbone pairs.

● Instead of using head pins to finish dangles, stitch small loops of seed beads above the cap-covered pearls.

● If you don't have bead stops, use tape to temporarily hold the pearls on the wires in Step 4. Painter's tape is less likely to leave behind a sticky residue.

## DESIGN OPTIONS

● Make a gorgeous pair of matching earrings by using an etched jump ring to attach 3 dangles to a brass ear wire; repeat for a second earring.

● The bead caps are also beautiful in shades of blue, seafoam green, and topaz. Gold size 15°s were used at the tip of each herringbone column to match the gold finish of this bracelet's textured chain. Teal faceted 7mm round pearls fill each bead cap and also hang from the chain as additional dangles, alongside topaz/green 5mm potato-pearl dangles.

The hidden closure was made with a gold-plated steel 6×12mm (with 1mm hole and 2.4×2mm inner well) heavy-duty strength magnetic barrel clasp. To assemble, pass the end of 1 flat-end head pin through the center of one half of the clasp, string 1 bead cap (wide end first) down over the top of the clasp, and form a wrapped loop that attaches to one end of the chain; repeat at the other end of the chain.

Discover how right-angle weave makes a great foundation for peyote stitch in this classic earring-and-bracelet set. The circular right-angle-weave starting round is flexible and thus creates a perfect fit for shaped crystal fancy stones such as the irresistible blue squares used here. A unique combination of colors and materials give this set a vintage feel. • *by melinda barta*

# on broadway beauties

### TECHNIQUES
Tubular and circular peyote stitch

Circular and flat right-angle weave

Square stitch

### TOOLS
Scissors or thread burner

Size 10 and 12 beading needles

2 pairs of chain- or flat-nose pliers

### FINISHED SIZE
2¼" (5.7 cm) (earrings); 7¼" (18.4 cm) (bracelet)

## EARRINGS
### MATERIALS

.5 g cobalt gold luster size 15° Japanese seed beads (A)

1 g dark steel/silver sage permanent galvanized size 11° Japanese seed beads (B)

1 g light bronze metallic size 11° cylinder beads (C)

1 g raspberry metallic size 11° cylinder beads (D)

40 cyclamen opal 2mm crystal rounds (E)

8 cyclamen opal 3mm crystal bicones (F)

2 foil-backed Titan blue 12mm pointed-back crystal square fancy stones

2 natural brass 14×18mm filigree 2-to-1 links

2 antique copper 3×4mm oval jump rings

1 pair of antique brass ⅝" (1.6 cm) ear wires

1¾" (4.4 cm) of antique copper 2×2.5mm oval chain

Smoke 6 lb braided beading thread

Microcrystalline wax

**1 bezel.** Use circular right-angle weave and tubular peyote stitch to bezel a square crystal: **note:** *Start with the size 10 needle and switch to the size 12 if you ever have trouble fitting the needle through beads.*

**ROUND 1, UNITS 1–15** Use 4' (1.2 m) of waxed thread to string 4C; pass through the first 2C to form a circle. String 3C, then pass through the last C exited and the first 2 just added; repeat thirteen times for a total of 15 right-angle-weave units *(fig. 01)*.

**ROUND 1, UNIT 16** String 1C; pass through the side C of Unit 1 on

fig. 01: working units 1–15

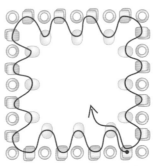

fig. 03: working round 2

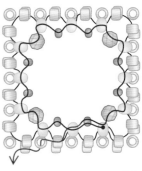

fig. 02: forming unit 16 to join the strip into a ring

fig. 04: stitching round 3 and exiting the bottom round 1

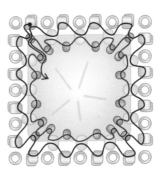

fig. 05: adding rounds 4 and 5 on the back of the bezel

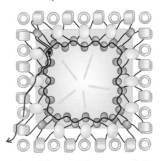

fig. 06: working round 6 and weaving through to the front of the bezel

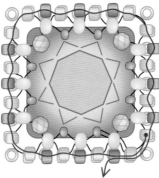

fig. 07: stitching the first embellishment round

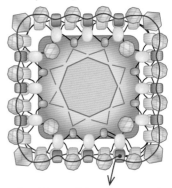

fig. 08: working the second embellishment round

mastering peyote stitch

the starting end of the strip. String 1C; pass through the nearest side C of Unit 15. Exit the top of the unit *(fig. 02)*.

**ROUND 2** String 1B and pass through the C at the top of the next unit of Round 1; repeat twice. Pass through the C at the top of the next unit of Round 1 without adding a bead to form a decrease. Repeat the entire sequence three times to add a total of 12B. **note:** *By skipping the corners you will cause the beadwork to take on a square shape to match the outline of the crystal stone.* Repeat the thread path and step up by exiting from the first B added in this round *(fig. 03)*.

**ROUND 3** Work 2 tubular peyote stitches with 1A in each stitch and 1 tubular peyote stitch with 1E; repeat this sequence three times to add a total of 8A and 4E *(fig. 04, blue)*. Use relaxed tension on the first pass around to avoid cutting your thread on the crystal rounds. Repeat the thread path using tighter tension. Weave through beads to exit a bottom C of Round 1, exiting toward a corner *(fig. 04, red)*.

**ROUND 4** Flip the beadwork over. String 1A; pass through the next C of Round 1. String 1B and pass through the next C of Round 1; repeat twice. Repeat the entire sequence three times to add a total of 4A and 12B. Repeat the thread path. Insert 1 crystal stone so Rounds 1–3 rest against the face of the crystal stone. Pull the thread to snug the beadwork

around the crystal stone. Step up through the first bead added in this round *(fig. 05, blue)*. **note:** *You are now working counterclockwise around the back of the bezel.*

**ROUND 5** Work tubular peyote stitch with 1A in each stitch to add a total of 16A. Step up through the first bead added in this round *(fig. 05, red)*.

**ROUND 6** Work 3 tubular peyote stitches with 1A in each stitch and, without adding a bead, pass through the next A of Round 5 to form a decrease; repeat three times to add a total of 12A. Step up through the first bead added in this round *(fig. 06, blue)*. Weave through beads to exit a top C of Round 1, exiting toward a corner *(fig. 06, red)*.

**ROUND 7 (EMBELLISHMENT)** Flip the bezel over so the crystal is now faceup. **note:** *You are now*

*working clockwise again around the front of the bezel.* *Pass through the top of the next unit of Round 1 without adding a bead to form a decrease. String 1D and pass through the C at the top of the next unit of Round 1; repeat twice. Repeat from * three times to add a total of 12D. Weave through beads to exit the first bead added in this round *(fig. 07)*.

**ROUND 8 (EMBELLISHMENT)** String 1E and pass through the next D of Round 7; repeat. String 1E, 1F, and 1E and pass through the next E of Round 7. Repeat the entire sequence three times to add a total of 16E and 4F *(fig. 08)*. Use relaxed tension on the first pass around to avoid cutting your thread on the crystal round. Repeat the thread path at least once using tighter tension.

**2 assembly.** Attach the chains to the bezel and connect the earring findings:

**ATTACH CHAINS** Weave through beads to the back of the bezel, exiting from 1 bottom corner C with the needle pointing away from the corner. String 1A and one end of one ¾" (1.9 cm) piece of chain; pass through the next bottom C. Weave through beads to exit the mirror C of the one last exited on the adjacent side of the bezel. String one end of one ¾" (1.9 cm) piece of chain and 1A; pass through the next bottom C *(fig. 09, red)*. Repeat the thread path. Secure the thread and trim.

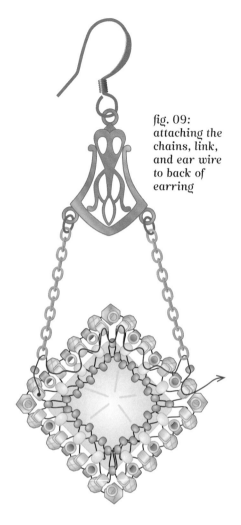

fig. 09: attaching the chains, link, and ear wire to back of earring

back of earring

**JUMP RINGS** Use 1 jump ring to attach one end of 1 chain to 1 loop on the bottom (2-loop end) of 1 link. Repeat to attach the other chain to the second bottom loop, making sure the chains aren't twisted and the front sides of the bezel and link face the same direction.

**EAR WIRE** Opening and closing the loop of the ear wire as you would a jump ring, attach the ear wire to the top of the link, making sure the earring faces forward when worn **(fig. 09)**.

Repeat Steps 1 and 2 for a second earring.

## BRACELET
### MATERIALS

2 g cobalt gold luster size 15° Japanese seed beads (A)

2 g dark steel/silver sage permanent galvanized size 11° Japanese seed beads (B)

3 g light bronze metallic size 11° cylinder beads (C)

1 g raspberry metallic size 11° cylinder beads (D)

180 cyclamen opal 2mm crystal rounds (E)

36 cyclamen opal 3mm crystals bicones (F)

9 foil-backed Titan blue 12mm pointed-back crystal square fancy stones

Smoke 6 lb braided beading thread

Microcrystalline wax

**1** **bezels.** Repeat Earrings Step 1 nine times for a total of 9 bezels, this time using 6' (1.8 m) of thread.

**2** **band connection.** Use flat right-angle weave to connect the bezels:

**ROW 1, UNIT 1** Weave the thread of 1 bezel through beads toward the back, exiting from the second bottom C from one corner. String 3C; pass through the C last exited on the bezel and the first C just strung **(fig. 10, blue)**.

**ROW 1, UNIT 2** String 2C; pass back through the next C on the bezel. Pass through the nearest C of Unit 1 and the first C added in this unit **(fig. 10, red)**. *Row 2, Unit 1:* String 1C; pass through the second bottom C from a corner on the back of a second bezel. String 1C; pass through the nearest C of Row 1, Unit 2, the first C added in this unit, the nearest C on the second bezel, and the second C added in this unit **(fig. 11, blue)**.

**ROW 2, UNIT 2** Pass through the nearest C of Row 1, Unit 1. String 1C; pass back through the next C on the second bezel. Pass through the nearest C of the Row 2, Unit 1 **(fig. 11, red)**.

**EMBELLISHMENT** Pass the needle between beads to exit toward the front of the bezels. String 1A; pass through the nearest 2C. String 1A; pass through next C; repeat around the outside edges of Rows 1 and 2 to add a total of 9A **(fig. 12)**. Secure the thread and trim.

Repeat this entire step six times to form a band of 8 bezels.

**3** **clasp connection strip.** Use flat right-angle weave to form a strip at one end of the band:

**ROW 1** Repeat Step 2, Row 1 at the end of the band. **note:** *Instead of weaving the thread of the last bezel added through beads to reach the C the band will start from, you may find it easier to start 18" (45.7 cm) of new thread.*

**ROW 2** String 3C; pass through the last C exited in the previous row, the 3C just added, and the next C of the previous row. String 2C; pass through the nearest C of the previous unit, the last C exited in the previous row, and the 2C just added *(fig. 13, purple)*.

**ROW 3** String 3C; pass through the last C exited in the previous row and the first C just added. String 2C; pass through the nearest C of the previous row, the last C exited in the previous unit, and the first C just added *(fig. 13, green)*.

**ROWS 4 AND 5** Repeat Rows 2 and 3 *(fig. 13, blue)*.

**EMBELLISHMENT** Repeat Step 2, Embellishment to add 1A between each C along the outside perimeter and down the centerline of the grid *(fig. 13, red)*. Secure the thread and trim.

**4** **clasp button.** Turn the remaining bezel into a clasp button and connect it to the strip formed in Step 3:

**BUTTON BACK** Weave through beads to exit the back of the bezel from 1A of Round 6 that is in the center of one side. **note:** *You may find it easier to start 1' (.3 m) of new thread instead of weaving through beads to reach the back*

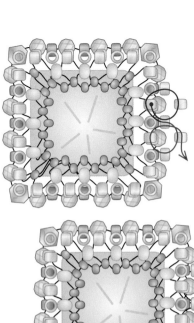

fig. 10: adding row 1, units 1 and 2 of the band connection

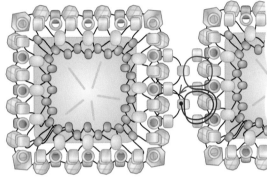

fig. 11: working row 2 and connecting to a second bezel

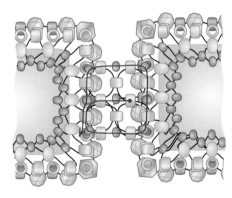

fig. 12: adding embellishments to the band connection [shown from back for clarity]

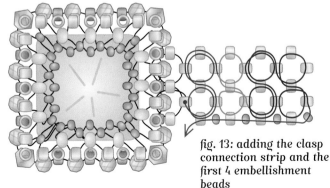

fig. 13: adding the clasp connection strip and the first 4 embellishment beads

*of the bezel.* String 4A, 1C, and 4A; pass through the mirror A of Round 6 on the opposite side of the bezel. Pass back through the 4A/1C/4A, then pass through the first A exited and the first 5 beads strung *(fig. 14, blue)*. String 4A; pass through the center A of Round 6 on an adjacent side of the bezel. Pass back through the 4A and through the C. String 4A; pass through the mirror A of Round 6 on the opposite side of the bezel. Pass back through the last 4A strung and through the C *(fig. 14, red)*.

**CONNECTION** Square-stitch the C on the back of the button to the center C of the front of the clasp connection strip's Row 5 *(fig. 15)*. Repeat the thread path twice to reinforce. Secure the thread and trim.

**5 clasp loop.** Use circular peyote stitch to form a clasp loop:

**ROUNDS 1 AND 2** Start 1' (.3 m) of new thread that exits from a bottom C on the back of the bezel that is at the opposite end of the band from the clasp button. String 35D; pass through the C of the other corner at the same end of the band *(fig. 16, green)*.

**END** String 1D and pass through the next C at the end of the band; repeat twice. Pass through the first C added in this step *(fig. 16, blue)*.

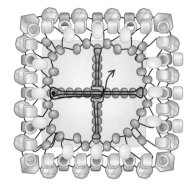

fig. 14: forming the back of the clasp button

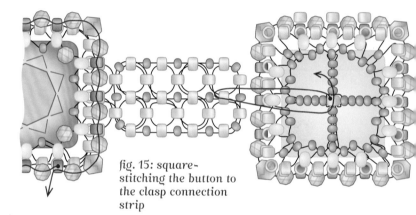

fig. 15: square-stitching the button to the clasp connection strip

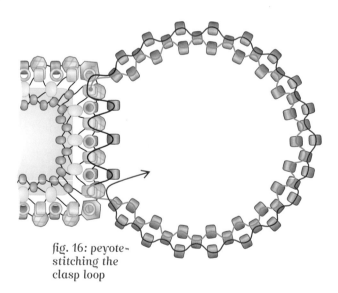

fig. 16: peyote-stitching the clasp loop

**ROUND 3** String 1D, skip 1D previously strung, and pass through the next D; repeat sixteen times to add a total of 17D *(fig. 16, red)*. Secure the thread and trim.

## TIPS

● The earrings shown mix natural brass links and ear wires with antique copper chain. Since the brass links are light in color this combination works well with the warm-hued bronze cylinder beads. If your copper chain looks too orange against the natural brass findings, change up the choice of metals to your liking.

● To easily make subtle size adjustments to the length of the bracelet, work more or fewer rows when creating the clasp connection strip in Step 3. If making more dramatic alterations, keep in mind one bezel and band connection equals ⅞" (2.2 cm).

● If you're concerned the foil backing on the fancy stones could scratch, coat the back of them with clear fingernail polish.

● After stringing the beads of the first right-angle-weave unit in Step 1, don't knot the threads to form a tight circle. By not tying a knot, you'll leave a little bit of give in the starting round. Any slack between the Unit 1 beads can be removed when working Unit 16.

## DESIGN OPTION

### double-diamond earrings

A variation of the On Broadway Beauties, these striking double-diamond post earrings showcase two techniques for bezeling the crystal square stones. Repeat the instructions on pages 130 and 131 to bezel one with right-angle weave (with the following color changes) and bezel the other with tubular peyote stitch.

### MATERIALS

.5 g teal purple gold luster size 15° Japanese seed beads

.5 g silver gray opaque gold luster size 15° Japanese seed beads

1 g smoked gray opaque gold luster size 11° Japanese seed beads

2 g palladium electroplate size 11° cylinder beads

1 g blue-green metallic gold iris size 11° cylinder beads

48 Montana blue 2mm crystal rounds

8 aquamarine satin 3mm crystal bicones

2 foil-backed white opal 10mm pointed-back crystal square fancy stones

2 foil-backed white opal 12mm pointed-back crystal square fancy stones

1 pair of sterling silver post earrings with 4mm balls

1 pair of sterling silver 5mm earring backs

Smoke 6 lb braided beading thread

**1** **large bezel.** Use circular right-angle weave and tubular peyote stitch to bezel a square crystal. Unless otherwise noted, repeat instructions for Step 1 (bezel) of the On Broadway Beauties earrings and use the following color changes:

**ROUND 1, UNITS 1–16** Use palladium cylinders in place of C.

**ROUND 2** Use gray size 11°s in place of B.

**ROUND 3** Use teal size 15°s in place of A and Montana blue 2mm rounds in place of E.

**ROUND 4** Use teal size 15°s in place of A and gray size 11°s in place of B.

**ROUND 5** Use teal size 15°s in place of A.

**ROUND 6** Use teal size 15°s in place of A *(fig. 17, blue)*.

**CONNECTION BEAD** Weave through beads to exit 1 bottom palladium cylinder of Round 1 on the back of the bezel, exiting toward a corner. String 1 blue-green cylinder; pass through the following bead of Round 1 and weave through beads to exit a top bead of Round 1, exiting toward a corner *(fig. 17, red)*. note: *The blue-green cylinder will connect this bezel to the next during assembly.*

**ROUND 7 (EMBELLISHMENT)** Use blue-green cylinders in place of D.

**ROUND 8 (EMBELLISHMENT)** Use Montana blue 2mm rounds in place of E and aquamarine 3mm bicones in place of F.

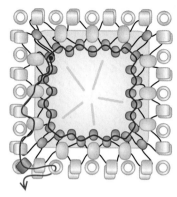

fig. 17: adding the connection bead for the double-diamond earrings

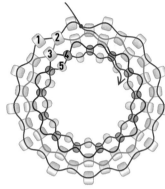

fig. 18: working rounds 1–5 of the small bezel

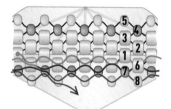

fig. 19: stitching rounds 6–8

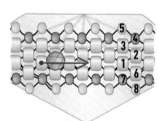

fig. 20: adding a 2mm crystal to round 1

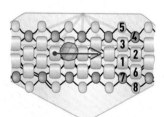

fig. 21: adding a 2mm crystal to round 2

fig. 22: assembling the earring [back view]

**2 small bezel.** Use tubular peyote stitch to bezel the small square crystal stone:

**ROUNDS 1 AND 2** Use 5' (1.5 m) of thread to string 26 palladium cylinders, leaving a 10" (25.4 cm) tail. Tie a square knot with the tail and working threads to form a ring, leaving one bead's width of space so the ring is not too tight. Pass through the first bead strung, making sure the knot doesn't slip inside the bead *(fig. 18, purple)*.

**ROUND 3** String 1 palladium cylinder, skip 1 bead previously strung, and pass through the next bead; repeat twelve times to add a total of 13 palladium cylinders *(fig. 18, green)*. note: *Step up for each new round by passing through the first bead added in the current round.*

**ROUND 4** Work 1 teal size 15° in each stitch to add a total of 13 teal size 15°s *(fig. 18, blue)*. Use tight tension to cause the beadwork to cup.

**ROUND 5** Work 1 gray size 15° in each stitch to add a total of 13 gray size 15°s *(fig. 18, red)*. Weave through beads to exit Round 1. Insert 1 crystal stone so the previous rounds rest against the face of the crystal stone. Hold the crystal stone firmly in place as you work the following rounds. Using tight tension in Rounds 7 and 8 will help the circular cup of peyote take on the square profile of the crystal stone.

**ROUND 6** Work off Round 1 with 1 palladium cylinder in each stitch to add a total of 13 palladium cylinders *(fig. 19, green)*. Use tight tension to cause the beadwork to cup.

**ROUND 7** Work 1 teal size 15° in each stitch to add a total of 13 teal size 15°s *(fig. 19, blue)*.

**ROUND 8** Work 1 gray size 15° in each stitch to add a total of 13 gray size 15°s *(fig. 19, red)*.

**EMBELLISHMENT** Weave through beads to exit a palladium cylinder of Round 1 or Round 2 near 1 corner of the bezel. String 1 Montana blue 2mm round; pass through the next bead of the current round. note: *The 2mm round can be attached to Round 1 (fig. 20) or Round 2 (fig. 21), choose the round that best places the 2mm round at the corner.* Weave through beads to reach the next corner and repeat to add one 2mm round at each of the 4 corners. Use relaxed tension on the first pass around to avoid cutting your thread on the crystal rounds. Repeat the thread path at least once using tighter tension. Exit from one 2mm round.

**3 assembly.** Connect the small and large bezels to an ear post to finish the earring:

**BEZEL CONNECTION** String 3 gray size 15°s; pass through the blue-green connection bead on the large bezel to form a picot. String 3 gray size 15°s; pass through the last 2mm round exited and the first gray size 15° added to form a second picot. Skip 1 gray size 15°; pass through the next gray size 15°, connection cylinder, and gray size 15°. Skip 1 gray size 15°; pass through the next gray size 15° and 2mm round *(fig. 22, blue)*. note: *Use tight tension on the second pass to make the center gray size 15° of each picot "pop" out.* Secure the thread and trim.

**EARRING CONNECTION** Add a needle to the small bezel's tail thread and weave through beads to exit the 2mm round opposite the one just used in the bezel connection. Repeat to make 2 picots as for the bezel connection, this time connecting the loop of 1 ear post to the last 2mm round exited *(fig. 22, red)*. Secure the thread and trim. Repeat Steps 1–3 for a second earring.

# finishing touches

A little embellishment goes a long way, giving every peyote project an essential final touch. From fringe and picots to whipstitch and rope edgings, the finishing touches added to the projects that follow take each piece one perfectly detailed step further.

The rivolis in my **Zigzag Zing** bracelet start with classic tubular-peyote bezels and then stitch-in-the-ditch embellishments are carefully placed to give each component a striped pattern. Even the coordinating toggle ring is patterned to show another application for this type of embellishment.

Lisa Kan is well known for her romantic beadwork formed with rich layers of detailed embellishment. Her **Trésor** necklace is no exception, featuring circular- and tubular-peyote–stitched components decorated with picots and a rope edging.

*A few decorative stitches easily add richness and intricate details to every design.*

## TECHNIQUES

### fringe

Simple to stitch, fringe is one of the most common embellishments used by beadweavers.

#### basic fringe

To form a fringe, string 1 or more decorative beads and 1 bead for the tip, then pass back through the decorative bead(s) *(fig. 01, blue)*. If using crystals for the decorative beads, consider stringing 1 small bead before the crystal *(red thread)*. This will help protect the thread from accidental cutting.

To tighten the fringe, pull up on the bead at the tip to snug the decorative bead down to the beadwork, and then pull the thread to remove the rest of the slack.

#### loop fringe

Here, decorative loops of beads are added to the end of a peyote strip. To add loops to the side of a flat peyote piece, see the rope edging below. Work the loops by stringing any number of beads, skipping over a few beads at the end of the final row/round, and passing through the next end bead. Adjust the number of beads in each loop and the number of beads skipped in the final row/round to achieve the desired look *(fig. 02)*. Many of the thread paths used for the picot variations that follow will also work for loop fringe—just work each stitch with more beads. You may also hear a loop of beads referred to as a net.

### stitch-in-the-ditch embellishment

Layers of decoration can be easily added to previously stitched rows/ rounds of beadwork. Exit 1 bead in the row/round you wish to embellish, string 1 decorative bead, and pass through the next bead in the same row/round. Repeat as desired *(fig. 03)*.

### picot embellishment

There are many varieties of picots, and their common characteristic is that each is made with 3 beads. They are most often used for decorative edgings.

#### basic picot

Peyote-stitch the final row/round of any flat, circular, or tubular peyote project with 3 beads in each stitch. Use tight tension so the center bead juts out from the other 2 *(fig. 04)*.

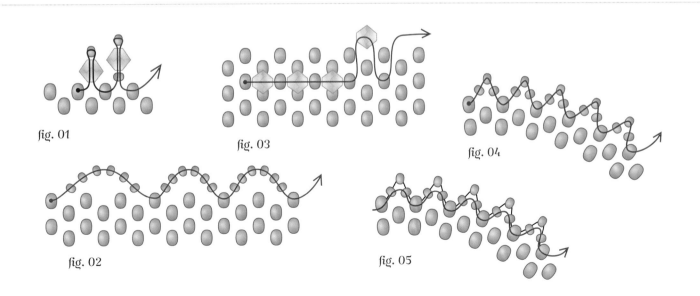

fig. 01

fig. 03

fig. 04

fig. 02

fig. 05

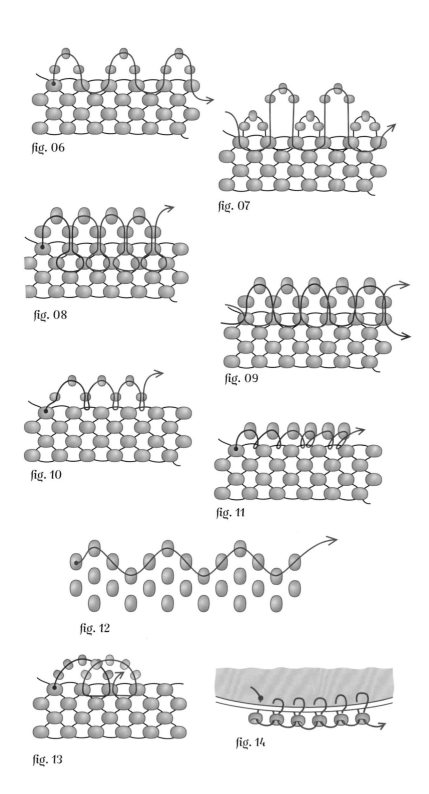

fig. 06

fig. 07

fig. 08

fig. 09

fig. 10

fig. 11

fig. 12

fig. 13

fig. 14

To make the tip even more defined, work a second pass through the beads, skipping the center bead of the picot *(fig. 05)*.

## picot edging

Choose from the following methods when edging the border of your beadwork with picots.

### basic picot

To add picots along the side of a strip of beadwork, exit away from the beadwork from 1 edge bead. String 3 beads, pass down through the next edge bead and up through the next. Repeat along the edge *(fig. 06)*.

To add twice the number of picots, work a second pass along the same edge. Place these picots between those previously added *(fig. 07)*.

### interlocking picots

Try this variation to create an edging that is a bit stiffer than the previous method. Notice each new picot shares a bead with the previous one. For the first stitch, string 3 beads, and pass through the next edge bead. Work a turnaround so you can pass back through the last edge bead exited and the last bead strung *(fig. 08, blue)*. To work the following stitches, string 2 beads, pass through the next edge bead, and work a turnaround as before to pass back through the last edge bead exited, and the last bead strung *(fig. 08, red)*.

Another way to achieve this look is by working 2 passes. Work the first pass with basic picots *(fig. 09,* blue). Work a second pass, passing back through the third bead of the first picot to start. For the following stitches, string 1 bead, pass back through the first bead of the next picot, the 2 nearest edge beads, and back through the last bead of the next picot *(fig. 09, red)*.

### brick-stitch picots

You can also use brick stitch to work a picot edging. Choose this variation if the size of the picot beads varies significantly from the size of the beads in the body of the work. This is because brick stitch allows you to add more or fewer stitches to the thread loops along the sides of the beadwork. But since these beads are only attached to the threads of the peyote-stitch base, the two previous variations will feel more secure than this one. For the first stitch, string 3 beads, skip 1 bead along the edge, pass the needle under the next thread loop, and pass back through the last bead added to form a brick stitch *(fig. 10, blue)*. To work the following stitches, string 2 beads, pass the needle under the next thread loop, and pass back through the last bead added to form another brick stitch *(fig. 10, red)*.

### whipstitch edging

To add a low-profile edging, start by exiting away from the beadwork from 1 edge bead. String 1 bead and pass the needle under the nearest thread loop on the side of the beadwork. Pull the thread to snug the bead against the edge of the

beadwork. Repeat along the edge *(fig. 11, blue)*. As with brick stitch, this edging allows you to use any size bead because you can change up the number of stitches attached to the thread loops *(fig. 11, red)*.

### peyote zigzag/peaked/scalloped edging

Give a plain edge a wavy finish by peyote-stitching 1 bead in every other stitch in the final row/round. When not adding a bead, form a decrease by weaving through the bead of the previous row/round. This works best if the total number of beads in the row/round is divisible by 4 (otherwise the last bead added will break the every-other-stitch pattern) *(fig. 12)*.

### rope edging

Form a series of overlapping loop fringes along an edge to create a ropelike border. Exit away from the beadwork from 1 edge bead. String 5 (or more) beads, skip 1 edge bead, pass down through the next, and up through the skipped edge bead *(fig. 13, blue)*. Repeat along the edge, making sure each new loop formed sits on top of the previous one *(fig. 13, red)*.

To see rope edging worked on the end of a circular peyote–stitch piece of beadwork, see Lisa Kan's Trésor necklace on page 150.

### basic brick-stitch edging

Add brick stitches along the border of your next bead-embroidered project to give the design a professional finish. In addition to being decorative, the stitches also help join and secure the layers of beading foundation and backing material. See Step 5 of Sherry Serafini's Marcella Cuff (page 78) for how-to. This technique is similar to the edging with brick-stitch picots above, but each stitch only contains 1 bead *(fig. 14)*.

Use tubular peyote stitch to bezel sparkling crystal rivolis and stitch-in-the-ditch embellishments to add color and texture. Embellishments, designed so that same-colored beads line up to create stripes, are added before the crystal is set to save time and avoid the frustration of stitching in tight places. Finish this dazzling bracelet by joining the elements in a fun-and-funky zigzag pattern. ● *by* *melinda barta*

# zigzag zing

## TECHNIQUES
Tubular, circular, and flat peyote stitch

Picot

Stitch-in-the-ditch embellishment

Zipping

## MATERIALS
2 g silver-lined smoky topaz AB size 15° Japanese seed beads (A)

4 g olive gold matte metallic iris size 15° Japanese seed beads (B)

7 g purple rose metallic gold iris size 11° cylinder beads (C)

2 g metallic olive green size 11° Japanese seed beads (D)

2 tourmaline 3mm crystal bicones

7 foil-backed purple haze 18mm crystal rivolis

Smoke 6 lb braided beading thread

## TOOLS
Size 10 and 12 beading needles

Scissors or thread burner

## FINISHED SIZE
7" (17.8 cm)

## NOTE
*The instructions are given for the pink colorway. For the gold-and-clear variation, see page 146.*

143

**1 bezel front.** Use tubular peyote stitch to work the front of the bezel: **note:** *Start with the size 10 needle and switch to the size 12 if you ever have trouble fitting the needle through beads.*

**BEZEL ROUNDS 1 AND 2** Use 5' (1.5 m) of thread to string 46C, leaving a 6" (15.2 cm) tail. Tie a square knot with the tail and working threads to form a circle, leaving 1 bead's width of space so the circle is not too tight. Pass through the first bead strung, making sure the knot doesn't slip inside the bead **(fig. 01, blue)**.

**BEZEL ROUND 3** String 1C, skip 1C previously strung, and pass through the next C; repeat to add a total of 23C **(fig. 01, red)**. **note:** *Unless otherwise noted, step up for each new round by passing through the first bead added in the current round.*

**BEZEL ROUND 4** Work 1B in each stitch to add a total of 23B **(fig. 02, blue)**. Use tight tension to cause the beadwork to cup.

**BEZEL ROUND 5** Work 1A in each stitch to add a total of 23A. Don't step up; exit Bezel Round 3 **(fig. 02, red)**. Secure the tail thread and trim.

**2 bezel embellishments.** Use circular peyote stitch to add stitch-in-the-ditch embellishments to the previous rounds:

**EMBELLISHMENT ROUND 1** Work off Bezel Round 3 with 1B in each stitch to add a total of 23B.

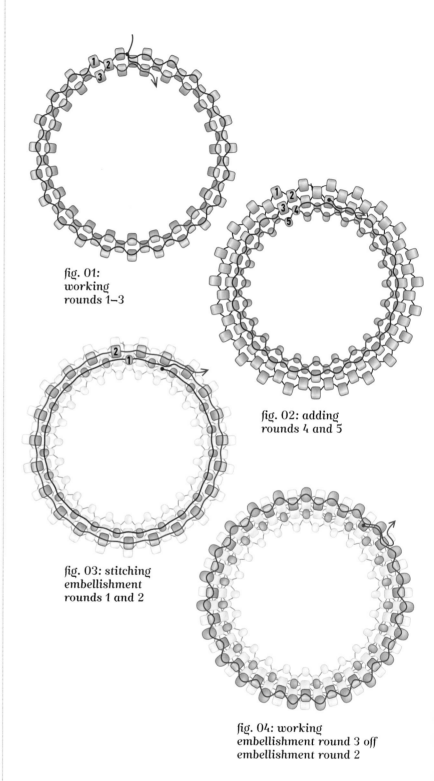

fig. 01:
working
rounds 1–3

fig. 02: adding
rounds 4 and 5

fig. 03: stitching
embellishment
rounds 1 and 2

fig. 04: working
embellishment round 3 off
embellishment round 2

Weave through beads to exit a bead of Bezel Round 2 *(fig. 03, blue)*.

**EMBELLISHMENT ROUND 2**
Work off Bezel Round 2 with 1C in each stitch to add a total of 23C. Exit the first C added in this round *(fig. 03, red)*.

**EMBELLISHMENT ROUND 3**
Work off Embellishment Round 2 with 1D in each stitch to add a total of 23D. Exit 1C of Embellishment Round 2 and pass back through the nearest C of Bezel Round 1 to form a turnaround *(fig. 04)*. **note:** *This will change the stitching direction. When looking at the front of the bezel, the thread will exit to the left, in a counterclockwise direction.*

**3 bezel back.** Use tubular peyote stitch to encase the rivoli and work the back of the bezel:

**BEZEL ROUND 6** Flip the work over. Work off Bezel Round 1 with 1C in each stitch to add a total of 23C *(fig. 05, blue)*. Insert 1 rivoli so the previous rounds rest against the face of the rivoli. **note:** *When holding the beadwork with the back of the rivoli facing you, you'll be working in a clockwise direction.*

**BEZEL ROUNDS 7 AND 8** Work 1A in each stitch to add a total of 23A in each of 2 rounds. Work with firm tension to keep the beadwork tight,

bezeling the rivoli in place. Don't step up; weave through beads to exit Bezel Round 6 *(fig. 05, red)*. **note:** You should still be traveling in a clockwise direction when looking at the back of the bezel. If you are not, work a turnaround to exit the right side of a Bezel Round 6 bead.

**4 connection strip.** Use flat peyote stitch to form a connection strip:

**ROW 1** Work 2 stitches with 1C in each stitch to add a total of 2C.

**ROWS 2-8** Continue working with 1C in each stitch to form a strip 4 beads wide and 8 rows long *(fig. 06)*. Remove the needle but don't trim the thread. Set the bezeled rivoli aside.

Repeat Steps 1–4 six times for a total of 7 bezeled rivolis with embellishments and connection strips.

**5 clasp ring.** Use tubular peyote stitch to form a clasp ring by stitching 2 sides off a central ring, zipping the sides together along the outside edge, and adding stitch-in-the-ditch embellishments:

**RING ROUNDS 1 AND 2** Use 5' (1.5 m) of thread to string {1A and 1B} twenty-three times for a total of 46 beads, leaving a 6" (15.2 cm) tail. Tie a square knot with the tail and working threads to form a circle, leaving 1 bead's

fig. 05: stitching bezel rounds 6–8 on the back of the rivoli

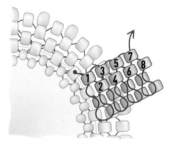

fig. 06: adding a connection strip

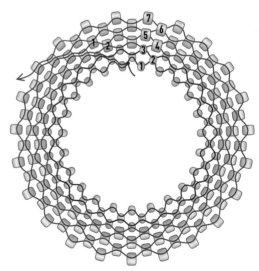

fig. 07: stitching the first side of the toggle ring

145

## MATERIALS

2 g 24k gold electroplate size 15°
Japanese seed beads

1 g amber/purple iris size 15° charlottes

5 g palladium electroplate size 11°
cylinder beads

2 g light aqua/bronze lined AB size 11°
Japanese seed beads

2 dorado 3mm crystal bicones

6 foil-backed clear 18mm crystal rivolis

Crystal 6 lb braided beading thread

## DESIGN OPTION

In the pink-and-green version, I added embellishments before setting the rivoli. However, some beaders prefer to add embellishments after the rivoli is completely bezeled. If you go this route, don't work the bezel with tight thread tension, or it may be hard to pass through the beads when embellishing. The benefit of working embellishments as your final step is that you don't have to make up your mind at the start of the design—you can decide which colors and textures to add after the bezels are complete.

After you get a hang of the pink-and-green version, try this alternate order of embellishing. Follow the instructions for the pink-and-green version, but with these color and order-of-stitching changes:

**1 bezel front.** Work Bezel Rounds 1–3 with palladium cylinders. Work Bezel Rounds 4 and 5 with gold size 15°s.

**2 bezel back.** Bead the back of the bezel before adding embellishments: Work Bezel Round 6 with gold size 15°s and insert 1 clear rivoli. Work Bezel Rounds 7 and 8 with gold size 15°s.

**3 embellishments.** Work stitch-in-the-ditch embellishments off Bezel Round 3 with 1 charlotte in each stitch. Work stitch-in-the-ditch embellishments off Bezel Round 2 with 1 aqua size 11° in each stitch.

**4 connection strip.** Add connection strips as before using palladium cylinders.

**5 clasp ring.** Work Rounds 1–3 with gold size 15°s. Work Rounds 4–10 with palladium cylinder beads. Work stitch-in-the-ditch embellishments off Round 5 with 1 charlotte in each stitch. Work stitch-in-the-ditch embellishments off Bezel Round 6 with 1 aqua size 11° in each stitch.

**6 toggle bar.** Work the toggle bar with palladium cylinder beads. Finish the ends with dorado crystal bicones and picots made of charlottes and aqua size 11°s.

**7 assembly.** Join the bezeled rivolis as before, using gold size 15°s for the picots.

width of space so the circle is not too tight. Pass through the first 2 beads strung to exit 1B, making sure the knot doesn't slip inside a bead *(fig. 07, purple)*.

**RING ROUND 3** String 1A, skip 1A previously strung, and pass through the next B; repeat to add a total of 23A *(fig. 07, blue)*. note: *Unless otherwise noted, step up for each new round by passing through the first bead added in the current round. To keep the beadwork flexible, use relaxed thread tension.*

**RING ROUNDS 4-7** Work 1C in each stitch to add a total of 23C in each of 4 rounds *(fig. 07, red)*. note: *Work with slightly tighter thread tension in Ring Rounds 6 and 7 so the beadwork cups.* Weave through beads to exit Round 1.

**RING ROUNDS 8-10** Work 1C in each stitch to add a total of 23C in each of 3 rounds, working the first round off Ring Round 1 *(fig. 08)*. Hold the beadwork so that the beads added for this second side are inside the cup of beadwork. As you work this side, manipulate the beads with your thumb and index finger to encourage the cupping of the beadwork. The sides will curl up toward each other.

**ZIP** Fold the sides up toward each other so that Ring Round 7 meets Ring Round 10 and zip the edges together *(fig. 09)*. Repeat the thread path to reinforce. Exit 1C of Ring Round 7.

**RING EMBELLISHMENT ROUND 1** Work off Ring Round 7 with 1D in each stitch to add a total

of 23D. Don't step up; weave through beads to exit a bead of Ring Round 5 *(fig. 10, blue)*.

**RING EMBELLISHMENT ROUND 2** Work off Ring Round 5 with 1B in each stitch to add a total of 23B *(fig. 10, red)*. Secure the threads and trim.

**6 toggle bar:** Use flat peyote stitch to form a beaded tube, embellish the ends, and add a connecting strip:

**TUBE** Use 3' (.9 m) of thread and C to work a strip 18 beads wide and 12 rows long, leaving an 8" (20.3 cm) tail. Fold the ends toward each other so Row 1 meets Row 12 and zip the edges together.

**PICOTS** Weave through beads to exit 1 end C. String 3B, pass down through the next end C, and up through the following end C *(fig. 11, purple)*; repeat to add 2 more picots. Add a needle to the tail thread and add 3 picots in the same manner at the other end of the tube.

**BICONES** To exit the other end of the tube without weaving through all the beads, angle the needle to exit the center of the tube. String 1 bicone and 1A; pass back through the bicone and exit the other end of the tube. Repeat to add a bicone to the opposite end *(fig. 11, blue)*. Repeat the thread path to reinforce. Secure the tail thread and trim.

**STRIP** Add a needle to the working thread and weave through beads to exit the middle of the tube,

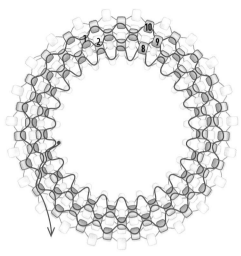

fig. 08: working the second side of the toggle ring

fig. 09: zipping the sides of the ring

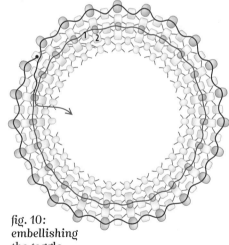

fig. 10: embellishing the toggle ring

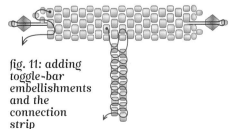

fig. 11: adding toggle-bar embellishments and the connection strip

147

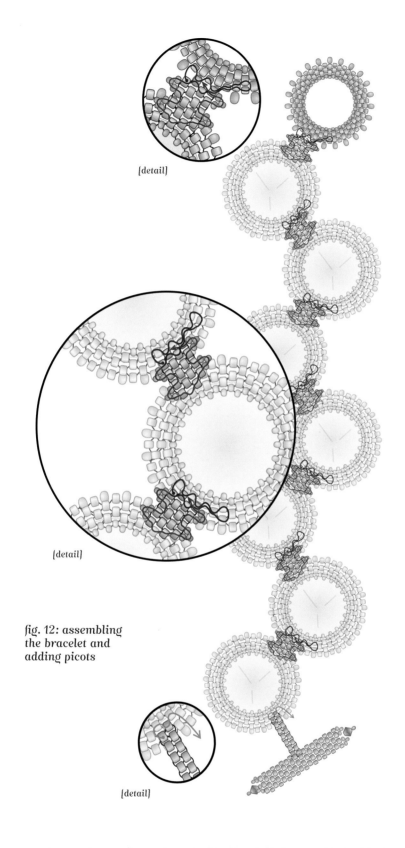

[detail]

[detail]

fig. 12: assembling
the bracelet and
adding picots

[detail]

8C from one end. String 1C, pass through the next C in the row last exited. Continue working with 1C in each stitch to form a strip 2 beads wide and 14 rows long *(fig. 11, red)*. Don't trim the thread. Set the toggle bar aside.

**7 assembly.** Join the bezeled rivolis, clasp ring, and toggle bar using the connection strips, and add picots:

**FIRST RIVOLI CONNECTION** Lay 2 bezeled rivolis facedown on your work surface. Add a needle to the first bezeled rivoli and zip the end of the strip to Bezel Round 6 of the next rivoli, referring to *fig. 12* for placement. Check the connection to make sure there are 5 beads of Bezel Round 6 between the 2 connection strips. Weave through beads of the bezel, work a turnaround, and weave back through beads to exit the opposite side of the strip *(fig. 12, blue)*.

**PICOTS** String 3A; pass down through the next edge C and up through the next. String 3A; pass down through the next edge C and weave through beads to exit the other side of the strip. Repeat this entire section to add picots along the other side of the strip *(fig. 12, red)*. Secure the thread and trim.

**SECOND RIVOLI CONNECTION** Attach a third bezeled rivoli in the same manner, this time pointing the connection strip in the other direction to establish the zigzag pattern; refer to *(fig. 12)* for placement. Again, check to be sure there are 5 beads of Round 6 between the 2 connection strips. Add picots as before.

Repeat this entire step until all the bezeled rivolis are connected. Attach the strip of the final rivoli to Ring Round 10 of the clasp ring, making sure the toggle-ring embellishments face the same direction as the bezeled-rivoli embellishments.

**TOGGLE-BAR CONNECTION** Zip the toggle-bar strip to the first

bezeled rivoli, leaving 6 beads of Round 6 between the 2 strips *(fig. 12, green)*. Add picots along each side of the strip as before.

## TIPS

● When working with different-sized rivolis, use this simple equation to determine how many Delica cylinder beads you'll need in your starting ring for Rounds 1 and 2: Multiply the size of the rivoli in millimeters by 2.5. For example, for a 12mm rivoli, multiply 12 by 2.5 for a total of 30 beads to be used for the starting ring (Rounds 1 and 2). If the total number is odd, add 1. For example, for an 18mm

rivoli, multiply 18 by 2.5 for a total of 45 beads; add 1 and use 46 beads for Rounds 1 and 2.

● For a bracelet 6½" (16.5 cm) long, work just 6 bezeled rivolis. For minor size adjustments, change the number of rows between each rivoli—just make sure each connection strip has an even number of rows. Or, lengthen the toggle-bar strip (again using an even number of rows); do not adjust the rows here to shorten the bracelet, or it may be hard to fit the toggle through the clasp ring.

## DESIGN OPTIONS

● Have a little fun with color. To maintain the striped effect, use the same color for A and C beads and a color that contrasts the A and C for the B and D beads.

You don't have to bezel just rivolis. Play around with buttons, coins, subway tokens, watch faces, and much more—including cabochons that are a bit more oval or square. Keep in mind you may need to experiment a little to find the perfect number of beads for the starting rounds and the number of rounds worked. At top, an 18mm pressed-glass cabochon was bezeled following the same basic pattern. An extra round of cylinders was worked to accommodate the cab's thick sides, and 3 extra rounds of size 15°s were worked on the back for security.

Inspired by the bead caps she designed for Aria Design Studio, Lisa created beautifully detailed, reversible components. The back of each cap contains a small crystal rivoli captured with peyote stitch. The fine embellishments prove that this elegant design that Lisa calls Trésor, French for treasure, truly lives up to its name. ● **by lisa kan**

# trésor

**TECHNIQUES**

Tubular and circular peyote stitch

Netting

Rope edging

Picot

Stitch-in-the ditch embellishment

Wirework

**MATERIALS**

5 g metallic bronze size 15° Japanese seed beads (A)

5 g metallic midnight blue size 15° Japanese seed beads (B)

5 g tanzanite teal luster size 15° Japanese seed beads (C)

5 g aqua violet luster size 15° Japanese seed beads (D)

5 g metallic bronze size 11° Japanese seed beads (E)

5 g transparent purple AB size 11° Japanese seed beads (F)

4 metallic blue 5mm crystal sequins

3 tabac 5mm crystal sequins

3 sage 5mm crystal sequins

3 foil-backed amethyst gold 14mm crystal rivolis

3 foil-backed tanzanite silver 14mm crystal rivolis

3 foil-backed Montana blue silver 14mm crystal rivolis

1 antique brass 2mm round

9 antique bronze 16.8mm Damask basket bead caps with 12-hole scalloped edge

1 antique brass 30x6mm engraved toggle bar

1 antique brass 1½" (3.8 cm) head pin

20 antique brass 24-gauge 4.75mm jump rings

2 antique brass 5.25mm jump rings

1" (2.5 cm) of antique brass 3.5x4mm unsoldered oval cable chain (8 links total)

7" (17.8 cm) of antique brass 5x7mm unsoldered oval chain (36 links total)

Smoke 6 lb braided beading thread

**TOOLS**

Size 12 needles

2 pairs of chain- or flat-nose pliers

Round-nose pliers

Wire cutters

Scissors

No-Tangle bobbin (optional)

**FINISHED SIZE**

18" (45.7 cm)

**TIPS**

● In lieu of the chain, change up the look of the necklace by stitching a beaded rope, making a Viking-knit strap, or using satin cording or silk ribbons.

● Any 14mm round stone similar in shape to the rivolis can be used as a substitute for the encapsulated crystal jewels.

151

**1 component.** Use seed beads, tubular peyote stitch, and netting to weave a bezel off the back of a bead cap and embellish with rope edging:

**SEQUIN** Use 3' (.9 m) of thread to string 1F; pass through the F twice more, leaving a 4" (10.2 cm) tail. Pass through the bead cap (wide end first), string 1 blue sequin (back to front), and 1A. Pass back through the sequin, bead cap, and 1F *(fig. 01, blue)*. String 1A; pass through all the beads and bead cap again to reinforce, exiting the 1A just added *(fig. 01, red)*. Tie 2 square knots with the working and tail threads. Trim the tail thread ⅛" (.3 cm) from the knot.

**ROUNDS 1 AND 2** Pass up through 1 edge scallop from back to front, string 1C, pass back through the same scallop. String 3D, pass up through the next edge scallop from back to front, string 1C, and pass back through the same scallop *(fig. 02)*; repeat eleven times. String 3D and step up through the first 1C and 3D added to add a total of 12C and 36D. Pass through all 36D added in this round *(fig. 03, blue)*.

**ROUND 3** String 1D, skip 1D, and pass through the next D; repeat to add a total of 18D. Step up through the first bead added in this round *(fig. 03, red)*.

**ROUND 4** Work tubular peyote stitch with 1D in each stitch to add a total of 18D. Step up through the first bead added in this round *(fig. 04, blue)*.

**ROUND 5** Repeat Round 4 with loose tension *(fig. 04, red)*. Insert 1 amethyst rivoli faceup inside the ring of D (with the foiled side against the inside of the cap). Pull the thread tight to cup the beadwork around the rivoli. Hold the rivoli in place with your thumb as you work the following rounds.

**ROUND 6** String 3A, skip 1D of Round 5, and pass through the next 1D; repeat eight times to add a total of nine 3A nets. Step up through the first 2A added in this round *(fig. 05, blue)*.

**ROUND 7** String 1A and pass through the center A of the next net of Round 6; repeat eight times to add a total of 9A *(fig. 05, red)*. Weave through beads to exit the right side of 1D of Round 2.

**SURFACE ROUND** String 1D and pass through the next D of Round 2; repeat stitching-in-the-ditch to add a total of 18D *(fig. 06)*. Step up through the first D added in this round.

**ROPE EDGING** Flip the beadwork over so the dome of the cap points up. *String 9B, skip 1D to

*rivoli side of components*

fig. 01: attaching the crystal sequin to the bead cap

fig. 02: stitching rounds 1 and 2 to the bead cap edging (looking toward inside of cap)

fig. 03: working round 3 inside the bead cap

fig. 04: stitching rounds 4 and 5

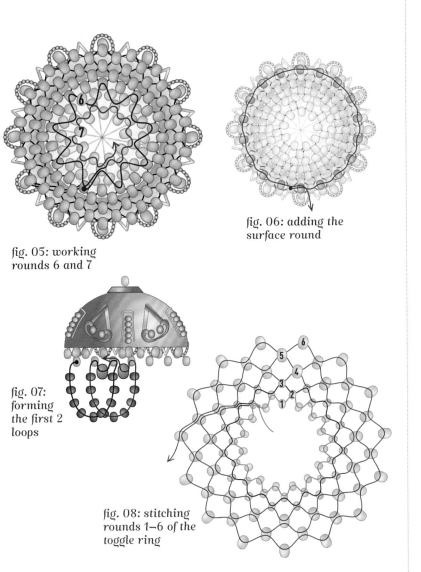

fig. 05: working
rounds 6 and 7

fig. 06: adding the
surface round

fig. 07:
forming
the first 2
loops

fig. 08: stitching
rounds 1–6 of the
toggle ring

Repeat this step three times using tabac sequins in place of the blue
sequins, D in place of C, B in place
of D, C in place of B, and tanzanite
rivolis in place of the amethyst
rivolis for a total of 3 tanzanite
components.

Repeat this step three times using sage sequins in place of the blue
sequins, B in place of C, C in place
of D, D in place of B, and Montana
rivolis in place of the amethyst
rivolis for a total of 3 Montana
components.

**2 toggle ring.** Create the
clasp ring with circular peyote
stitch and embellish it with rope
edging and picots:

**ROUNDS 1 AND 2** Use 5' (1.5 m) of
thread to string 30A, leaving a 2'
(.6 m) tail. Tie a square knot with
the tail and working threads to
form a circle. Pass through the
first A strung, making sure the
knot doesn't slip inside the bead
*(fig. 08, green)*. note: *You may
use a No-Tangle bobbin to keep the
tail thread out of your way for the
next few rounds.*

**ROUND 3** String 1A, skip 1A previously strung, and pass through
the next A; repeat fourteen times
to add a total of 15A. Step up
through the first A added in this
round *(fig. 08, blue)*.

**ROUNDS 4–6** Work circular peyote
stitch with 1E in each stitch to
add a total of 15E in each of 3
rounds, stepping up through
the first 1E added in each round
before starting the next round
*(fig. 08, red)*.

the right, and pass through the
next surface-round D with your
needle pointing back toward the
last bead exited. String 1F; pass
through the surface-round D just
skipped *(fig. 07, blue)*. Repeat
from * seventeen times to add
a total of 18 loops, making sure
each new loop rests on top of
the previous loop *(fig. 07, red)*.

Secure the thread and trim.
note: *When adding the last 2
loops, be aware that the orientation
of the loops should flow with the
beginning embellishments. You may
find it easier to turn the work back
over and work the final loop from
the underside.*

Repeat this step twice for a total
of 3 amethyst components.

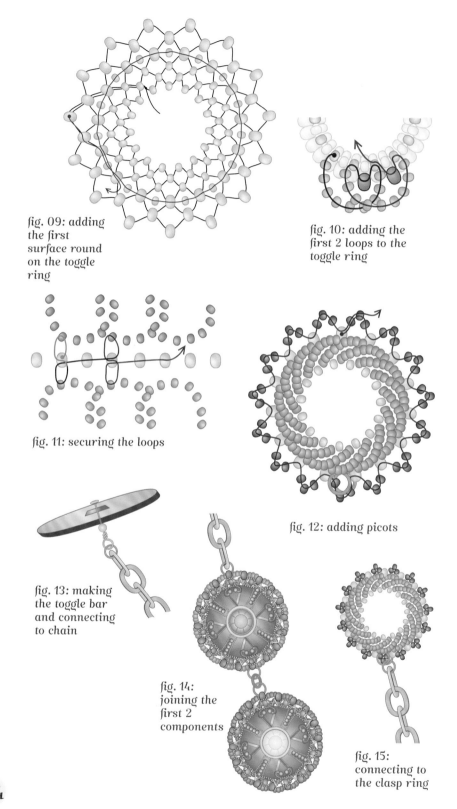

fig. 09: adding the first surface round on the toggle ring

fig. 10: adding the first 2 loops to the toggle ring

fig. 11: securing the loops

fig. 12: adding picots

fig. 13: making the toggle bar and connecting to chain

fig. 14: joining the first 2 components

fig. 15: connecting to the clasp ring

**SURFACE ROUNDS** Weave through beads to exit 1E of Round 4. String 1A and pass through the next E of Round 4; repeat stitching-in-the-ditch to add a total of 15A. Exit Round 4 toward the other side of the ring **(fig. 09)**. Repeat on the other side of the ring, stitching through the beads of Round 4 once again. Step up through the first 1A added in this round.

**ROPE EDGING** Check to make sure you're exiting to the left from a surface-round A; work a turnaround if needed. *String 9D, skip 1A to the right, and pass through the next surface-round A with your needle pointing back toward the last bead exited. String 1F; pass through the surface-round A just skipped **(fig. 10, blue)**. Repeat from * fourteen times to add a total of 15 loops, making sure each new loop rests on top of the previous **(fig. 10, red)**. note: *When adding the last 2 loops, be aware that the orientation of the loops should flow with the beginning embellishments.* Secure the thread and trim. Attach one 4.75mm jump ring to 1F to join to the chain later. Repeat this entire section to add rope edging to the surface round on the other side of the ring, using the tail thread and C in place of D. Don't trim the tail thread. When attaching the second 4.75mm jump ring, make sure it aligns with the location of the first jump ring so they can both be joined to the chain with the same 5.25mm jump ring.

**SECURING THE LOOPS** Weave through beads to exit 1E of Round 6, *pass through the fourth D of the nearest loop, and through the E just exited *(fig. 11, green)*. Pass through the fourth C of the nearest loop on the other side of the ring, the E just exited, the next E of Round 5, and the next E of Round 6 *(fig. 11, blue)*. Repeat from * around to secure each loop to 1E of Round 6 *(fig. 11, red)*.

**PICOT EDGE** Exiting 1E of Round 6, string 3B and pass through the next 1E of Round 6; repeat fourteen times to add a total of fifteen 3B picots. When you reach the jump rings, spread them apart to add a picot between them *(fig. 12)*. Secure the thread and trim.

**3** **assembly.** Create the toggle bar and assemble the components:

**TOGGLE BAR** Use the head pin to string 1 blue sequin (front to back), the toggle bar (front to back), and the brass round; form a wrapped loop. Use one 5.25mm jump ring to attach the wrapped loop to one end of one 3½" (8.9 cm) (18-link) piece of 5×7mm chain *(fig. 13)*.

**CHAIN LINKS** Disassemble the 3.5×4mm unsoldered oval cable chain, opening and closing the links as you would jump rings.

**COMPONENT LINKS** Use one 4.75mm jump ring to attach the other end of the toggle-bar chain to the F of 1 tanzanite component. *Use one 4.75mm jump ring to attach the F on the opposite side of the tanzanite component to one 3.5×4mm chain link. Use one 4.75mm jump ring to attach the 3.5×4mm chain link to 1F of 1 Montana component *(fig. 14)*. note: *If at any time you have trouble passing a 4.75mm jump ring through an F, choose an adjacent F for the connection instead of forcing the jump ring through. Keep in mind you'll need to pass through an F opposite the previous, so make sure that F can accept a jump ring as well; depending on the size of your F beads, you may need to rotate and test the components in order to find a fit.* Repeat from * seven times to link the remaining components in this order: amethyst, tanzanite, Montana, amethyst, tanzanite, Montana, and amethyst. When adding the second jump ring to the second Montana component, attach it 4F from the previous connection to form a V shape in the center of the necklace.

**CLASP RING** Use one 4.75mm jump ring to attach the final amethyst component to one end of the remaining 3½" (8.9 cm) (18-link) piece of 5×7mm chain. Use the remaining large jump ring to attach the other end of the chain to the two 4.75mm jump rings on the toggle ring *(fig. 15)*.

## TIPS

● Instead of connecting 4.75mm jump rings to the F beads, stitch loops of 9A that join the F beads to the 3.5×4mm unsoldered oval cable chain links. This opens the option for you to reinforce the round of rope edging. (As is, the F-bead connections would be difficult to reinforce because the bead holes only allow for one pass of thread and a jump ring.)

● The components in this design can also be easily converted to earrings. The reversible nature makes the modular components very versatile.

● Attach the jump rings in different locations on the F beads to change the neckline shaping.

● Use 4 to 5mm jump rings in place of the 3.5x4mm unsoldered oval cable chain.

● Here's another design idea: Replace a few of the Damask components with beaded rings, following the toggle ring pattern. Turn the ring into a component by simply attaching another pair of jump rings to the toggle ring, opposite the first pair.

## CONTRIBUTORS

### About the Author

**MELINDA BARTA** is editor of *Beadwork* magazine. When she's not beading, she loves spending time with her family in the Colorado outdoors. She is the author of the best-selling books *Custom Cool Jewelry* and *Hip to Stitch*, coauthor of *Mixed Metals* (Interweave, 2005–2009), and has filmed many instructional DVDs. Melinda has taught her craft at Penland School of Crafts, John C. Campbell Folk School, and at bead shows across the country; she has assisted workshops at Haystack Mountain School and Arrowmont School of Craft. Melinda has shared her love of beading, embroidery, and teaching on DIY, PBS, HGTV, Style, and local television networks. See her Custom Cool column in each issue of *Beadwork*. *Visit melindabarta.com.*

### Contributing Designers

**Jean Campbell** writes about, teaches, and designs beadwork. She has written and edited more than forty-five books, including *Steampunk Style Jewelry* and *Creating Glamorous Jewelry with Swarovski Elements* (Creative Publishing International, 2010). She is a Create Your Style Crystallized Elements Ambassador for the Swarovski Company, a contributor to BeadingDaily.com, and a featured designer on several television programs, including DIY's *Jewelry Making* and *Beads, Baubles, and Jewels*. Jean is the senior editor of *Beadwork* magazine and conducts lectures and teaches jewelry-making workshops throughout the United States. She lives in Minneapolis, Minnesota, with her family and a whole lot of beads. *Visit jeancampbellink.com.*

**Lisa Kan** is a beadweaver, jewelry designer, and glass artist. With an eye for color and textural balance, Lisa combines basic beading stitches with crystals, pearls, and seed beads to create designs imbued with dimension and depth. Her focus is on wearable, multipurpose, and modular component beadwork design. She developed Aria Design Studio, a line of metal components designed to be combined with beadwork. She is the author of *Bead Romantique: Elegant Beadweaving Designs* (Interweave, 2008). *Visit lisakan.com.*

**Carole Ohl** is a graphic designer by trade. Her love of beading began in 2004, when a bead shop moved into her neighborhood. Until that day, she did about any art form available, and so far, beadweaving has "stuck" longer than any other. She teaches her own beadweaving designs and loves to create and share new ways to put beads together. She is also a certified Zentangle instructor, which she says has only made her a better beader. She lives in Dayton, Ohio, with her husband, Daved, and their three kitties. *Visit openseedarts.blogspot.com.*

**Melanie Potter** travels nationally teaching her designs and is director at School of Beadwork. Her studio is on the central coast of California in the beautiful town of San Luis Obispo. Melanie's favorite inspiration for her beadwork designs comes from nature's beauty. She works in partnership with noted author and artist Carol Wilcox Wells in bringing their illustrated designs to beaders in kit form. *Visit melaniepotter.com and schoolofbeadwork.com.*

**Jean Power** is an award-winning jewelry designer who enjoys combining her love of beads, shape, and color in her work. Her work is often inspired by the beads and techniques she uses, resulting in a pared-down look with little embellishment but big impact. Jean has been beading for more than ten years, and her love of geometric motifs was sparked with her very first peyote project. While beading her contribution to this book, she discovered how to add corners to her beadwork, beaded her first triangle, and has never looked back! When she's not beading, Jean is writing about beading, teaching beading, buying beads, or competing in roller derby. *Visit jeanpower.com.*

**Cynthia Rutledge** has been sharing the art of beading for twenty years. Her focus is the use of off-loom beadweaving to create jewelry designs that have a contemporary but timeless elegance. Passionate about history, Cynthia incorporates historical perspective in almost all of her art, transporting the viewer of her work to the world of fourteenth- to eighteenth-century Europe and the Mediterranean. She teaches around the United States and internationally with the goal of keeping the art form of beading alive and well. *Visit cynthiarutledge.net.*

**Sherry Serafini** lectures and teaches throughout the United States and has won numerous awards for excellence in design. She has written articles for several well-known magazines, and her work has been featured on the covers of trade magazines and catalogs. Sherry is the coauthor of the *Art of Bead Embroidery* (Kalmbach, 2007), with artist Heidi Kummli; *Beading Across America* (Kalmbach, 2011), with Amy Katz and Paulette Baron; and author of *Sensational Bead Embroidery* (Lark Books, 2011). Her bead art is owned and worn by Steven Tyler of Aerosmith, American singer Fergie, and Grammy-winner Melissa Etheridge, to name a few. Sherry resides in Natrona Heights, Pennsylvania, with her two daughters, Erika and Nikki, and her Boston terrier, Bailey. *Visit serafinibeadedjewelry.com.*

## PROJECT RESOURCES

Check your local bead shop for the materials used in this book or contact the companies listed here (see page 158 for contact information). Remember, some beads and findings may be limited in availability; if the companies don't have the exact beads shown in this book, they will probably have something similar that will work just as well. Visit melindabarta.com for a list of bead colors and their numbers used in many of the projects.

### Buckle-Up Cuff
*by Carole Ohl (p. 32)*

Clover brand D-rings: CreateForLess and Jo-Ann Fabric and Craft Stores. Velcro Sticky Back hook-and-loop dot sets: Jo-Ann Fabric and Craft Stores. Seed beads, Toho triangles, and FireLine braided beading thread: Charlene's Beads.

### Walkin' After Midnight
*by Melinda Barta (p. 36)*

Swarovski pearls: FusionBeads.com. Dritz brand hook-and-eye set: Jo-Ann Fabric and Craft Stores. Seed beads: Beyond Beadery.

### Making Waves
*by Melinda Barta (p. 50)*

Thai silver rondelles: Ands Silver. Seed beads: Beyond Beadery. Flower-and-leaf clasp: Green Girl Studios.

### Big Sky Bracelets
*by Melinda Barta (p. 56)*

Seed beads and FireLine braided beading thread: Beyond Beadery. Cord: Leather Cord USA. Head pin: Rishashay.

### Patterned Petals
*by Melanie Potter (p. 62)*

Kits containing Swarovski chatons (article #1028), Nymo nylon beading thread, and all other materials: School of Beadwork.

### Marcella Cuff
*by Sherry Serafini (p. 74)*

Pressed-glass rectangles: York Novelty Imports. Alene's Tacky Glue: Michaels. Delica cylinder beads, Lacy's Stiff Stuff beading foundation, FireLine braided beading thread, E-6000 jeweler's adhesive, Swarovski sequins, similar cabochons, and all other beads and findings: Fire Mountain Gems and Beads.

### Geometry 101
*by Melinda Barta (p. 80)*

Striped Czech seed beads: Luna's Beads and Glass. All other Czech seed beads: Orr's Trading Co. FireLine braided beading thread and all seed beads: Beyond Beadery. Pewter rings and clasp: Green Girl Studios. Recycled green glass rings: Bronwen Heilman, Ghostcow Glassworks. Striped rings and discs: Atlantic Art Glass.

### Happy-Go-Lucky Links
*by Melinda Barta (p. 92)*

Lampwork beads by Sarah Moran: z-beads. FireLine braided beading thread and seed beads: Beyond Beadery.

### Daisy Girl
*by Jean Campbell (p. 104)*

Seed beads, Swarovski crystal pearls, FireLine braided beading thread, and SoftFlex beading wire: Beyond Beadery. Findings: Fire Mountain Gems and Beads.

### Urban Skyline
*by Jean Power (p. 110)*

Delica cylinder beads, Nymo nylon beading thread, and all other materials: Beads by Blanche. Neck wire: Stitchncraft Beads.

### Pi R-Squared Lariat
*by Cynthia Rutledge (p. 114)*

Swarovski custom-coated crystal beaded chain and kits containing the bead chain, Delica cylinder beads, Swarovski bicones, One-G nylon beading thread, and all other materials: Cynthia Rutledge.

### Beaujolais
*by Melinda Barta (p. 122)*

Seed beads and FireLine braided beading thread: Beyond Beadery. Beadalon beading wire, crimp beads, tube clasp, and pearls: FusionBeads.com. Barrel clasp: Fire Mountain Gems and Beads. Jump rings and chain: Lima Beads or Vintaj Natural Brass Co. Head pins: Rishashay.

### On Broadway Beauties
*by Melinda Barta (p. 128)*

Opal 10mm Swarovski square crystal fancy stones (article #4470): Mega Jewels. FireLine braided beading thread, Delica cylinder beads, and all other fancy stones and seed beads: Beyond Beadery. Similarly colored 10mm and 12mm fancy stones: Dreamtime Creations. Post earrings, earring backs, and Swarovski crystal rounds and bicones: FusionBeads.com. Vintaj link and ear wire: Vintaj Natural Brass Co. or FusionBeads.com. Chain and jump rings: Ornamentea.

### Zigzag Zing
*by Melinda Barta (p. 142)*

FireLine braided beading thread and Swarovski rivolis and bicones: Beyond Beadery and FusionBeads.com. Green seed beads: FusionBeads.com. Delica cylinder beads and all other seed beads: Beyond Beadery.

### Trésor
*by Lisa Kan (p. 150)*

Swarovski Lochrosen crystal sequins (article #3128) and rivolis: K. Gottfried. Swarovski rivolis and brass round: San Gabriel Bead Co. Vintaj metal findings: Vintaj Natural Brass Co. or FusionBeads.com. Damask bronze basket bead caps: Lisa Kan Designs/ Aria Design Studio. Seed beads: Out On A Whim. FireLine braided beading thread: Bass Pro Shops.

## START SHOPPING

Check your local bead shop or contact the companies below to purchase the materials used in this book. See Project Resources section on page 157 for a list of materials for each project.

**Ands Silver**
(323) 254-5250
andssilver.com

**Atlantic Art Glass**
PO Box 432
Ellsworth, ME 04605
(207) 664-0222
atlanticartglass.com

**Bass Pro Shops**
(800) 227-7776
basspro.com

**Beads by Blanche**
160 N. Washington Ave.
Bergenfield, NJ 07621
(201) 385-6225
beadsbyblanche.com

**Beyond Beadery**
PO Box 460
Rollinsville, CO 80474
(800) 840-5548
beyondbeadery.com

**Bronwen Heilman,
Ghostcow Glassworks**
bronwenheilman.com

**Charlene's Beads**
(760) 530-9436
cbbeads.com

**CreateForLess**
6932 SW Macadam Ave.,
Ste. A
Portland, OR 97219
(866) 333-4463
createforless.com

**Cynthia Rutledge**
PO Box 3666
Crestline, CA 92325
(909) 338-0296
cynthiarutledge.net

**Dreamtime Creations**
(417) 678-5748
dreamtimecreations.com

**Fire Mountain Gems
and Beads**
1 Fire Mountain Wy.
Grants Pass, OR 97526
(800) 355-2137
firemountaingems.com

**FusionBeads.com**
3830 Stone Wy. N.
Seattle, WA 98103
(888) 781-3559
fusionbeads.com

**Green Girl Studios**
PO Box 19389
Asheville, NC 28815
(828) 298-2263
greengirlstudios.com

**Jo-Ann Fabric and
Craft Stores**
(888) 739-4120
joann.com

**K. Gottfried**
558 Mineral Spring Ave.,
Ste. 103
Pawtucket, RI 02860
(800) 897-2323
kgottfriedinc.com

**Leather Cord USA**
509 Hickory Ridge Trl.,
Ste. 110
Woodstock, GA 30188
(877) 700-2673
leathercordusa.com

**Lima Beads**
(888) 211-7919
limabeads.com

**Lisa Kan Designs/Aria
Design Studio**
PO Box 80491
San Marino, CA 91118
lisakan.com
ariadesignstudio.com

**Luna's Beads and Glass**
416 Main St.
Frisco, CO 80424
(970) 668-8001
lunasbeads.com

**Mega Jewels**
megajewelsla@sbcglobal.net

**Melinda Barta**
melinda@melindabarta.com
melindabarta.com

**Michaels**
(800) 642-4235
michaels.com

**Ornamentea**
509 N. West St.
Raleigh, NC 27603
(919) 834-6260
ornamentea.com

**Orr's Trading Co.**
3422 S. Broadway
Englewood, CO 80113
(303) 722-6466
orrs.com

**Out On A Whim**
121 E. Cotati Ave.
Cotati, CA 94931
(707) 664-8343
whimbeads.com

**Rishashay**
PO Box 8271
Missoula, MT 59807
(800) 517-3311
rishashay.com

**San Gabriel Bead Co.**
325 E. Live Oak Ave.
Arcadia, CA 91006
(626) 447-7753
beadcompany.com

**School of Beadwork**
(805) 440-2613
schoolofbeadwork.com

**Stitchncraft Beads**
2 Chaldicott Barns,
Tokes Lane
Semley, Dorset SP7 9AW
United Kingdom
stitchncraft.co.uk

**Vintaj Natural Brass Co.**
PO Box 246
Galena, IL 61036
(815) 776-0481
vintaj.com

**York Novelty Imports**
10 W. 37th St.
New York, NY 10018
(800) 223-6676
yorkbeads.com

**z-beads**
z-beads@sbcglobal.net
z-beads.com

# INDEX

# *Weave your way* through these other beading resources from Interweave

**GETTING STARTED
WITH SEED BEADS**
(Paperback)
Dustin Wedekind
ISBN 978-1-59668-975-6
$14.95

**MASTERING BEADWORK**
A Comprehensive Guide to
Off-Loom Techniques
Carol Huber Cypher
ISBN 978-1-59668-013-5
$24.95

**SEED BEAD FUSION**
18 Projects to Stitch,
Wire, and String
Rachel Nelson-Smith
ISBN 978-1-59668-156-9
$24.95